THE TURBAN

THE TURBAN

A History from East to West

Chris Filstrup
and
Jane Merrill

REAKTION BOOKS

In Memory of Phoebe Merrill

Published by
Reaktion Books Ltd
Unit 32, Waterside
44–48 Wharf Road
London N1 7UX, UK
www.reaktionbooks.co.uk

First published 2025

Printed and bound in India by Replika Press Pvt. Ltd

A catalogue record for this book is available from the British Library

ISBN 978 1 83639 074 9

CONTENTS

Paul Poiret, turban with aigrette and brooch, 1912.

Introduction

As newly-weds we travelled to Iran to teach in an international school. Our travels began in 1969, and outside the modern part of Tehran, where we lived and taught, the country was exotic, especially in art, music and architecture. We were attracted to the colours, fabrics and styles of clothing, and saw how they were a source of the hippie togs then in fashion in the West. We could even buy sheepskin vests and wear them back home. We also wore horsemen boots, soft wool robes, scarves embroidered with metallic and silk thread, and baggy pants. For Jane a chador was de rigueur in some localities, but more captivating were the gorgeous dresses of indigenous women in western Iran. We developed an aesthetic that was already being experimented with back home.

Chris haunted bookstores in the old part of Tehran, while days off found Jane sitting on piles of carpets and drinking tea with our favourite carpet dealer, Daveed. We were both interested in the types of cotton used for skirt and dress fabrics and woollens of the local tailors of Western clothes. With John Wertime, a textile expert, we travelled to several villages and towns to watch women knot the carpets. They wore scarves on their heads, but not veils. The men wore a variety of caps; only mullahs and Mevlevi Sufis wore turbans. The modernization efforts of Reza Shah Pahlavi and his son Mohammad Reza Shah Pahlavi discouraged veils and turbans, except for clergy.

More than anywhere else we travelled, turbans in Afghanistan were common, well-worn in pastels mostly and a marker of how traditional the Afghan culture was. The first time we crossed the border east of Mashhad, we immediately came across a truck stop. Seated around a large, worn carpet, lorry drivers from Afghanistan, Pakistan, Turkmenistan, Uzbekistan and Tajikistan were exchanging currencies with a turbaned money-changer whose vest pockets bulged with money, mostly Iranian tomans, afghanis, Turkish lira and U.S. dollars. On the corners of the carpet some men gambled while others drank tea served by the nearby *chai-khaneh*. In Herat we stopped to watch a game of *bozkeshi*, which involved horsemen trying to carry the carcass of a goat (*boz*) over a goal line. The horsemen wore wide turbans with many folds and a tail hanging down the side or back. We bought a cut of dark fabric, cotton, requested by a New York friend who had attended our hippie wedding dressed in a cotton salwar kameez and turban, which he had unwound and waved as we drove off on our honeymoon.

WHY WRITE A BOOK ABOUT TURBANS? Two reasons. One, there are no books on the headdress, at least not in European languages. And two, researching the topic took us into the lives of many nations, ranging geographically from India to the Caribbean. We followed the turban as it made its way into international trade, Renaissance art, stories and contemporary fashions. We found turbans on the heads of the Magi, European royalty, an American First Lady, magicians and a TV personality.

A turban is a fairly narrow strip of fabric folded and wrapped around the head. The wrap starts on the side of the head and spirals to the top. The end of the strip is sometimes tucked out of sight and sometimes slipped through a side fold and left hanging to the side or back of the head. Traditionally, the fabric was cotton, linen or silk, but primarily cotton in different weights from sheer to two-sided to very firm rubia. Now turbans in the West may be of any fabric. The cotton came from Asia, the Mediterranean, Africa and the Americas, with certain places becoming famous for their turban cotton, such as Madras in the eighteenth century. The length of the fabric is significant. One text states that it should be long enough 'to tie up a prisoner'. The fourteenth-century traveller Ibn Battuta used his turban to tie himself to his saddle when feeling weary on his journeys. Turbans were voluminous enough to hide valuables such as rings and purses.[1]

The origin of the turban lies in a sparsely recorded past. The elaborate headdress of the statue of the Mesopotamian Prince of Gudea of circa 2100 BCE, which resides in the Louvre, seems to be made of 'curly-textured material', but whether this is a wrap or hat remains unclear. There is evidence that the kings of Judah and Israel wore something like a turban. The edition of the King James New Revised Standard Bible published in 2001 translates two Hebrew words as 'turban': *mitznefet*, which has a root word sense of 'to wrap'; and *tvulim*, which in Ezekiel appears in the phrase *sorchie tvulim* with the sense of a turban with a tail, such as is commonly worn today in Afghanistan. This Bible translates these two Hebrew words as 'turban' in its descriptions of priestly vestments, for example, Exodus 28:37–9 and Zechariah 3:5. In Job 29:14, Ezekiel 23:15 and Isaiah 3:23, 'turban' describes secular clothing worn by both the Israelites and by foreigners, such as the Babylonians who ruled over the Jews held in captivity.[2] As with her Egyptian forebears, Cleopatra had nothing like a turban in her clothes chest.

The translators who created the King James Bible in the early 1600s did not use the word 'turban'. Rather they used 'mitre', 'diadem', 'attire' and even 'bonnet' to render into English these two Hebrew words and the various Latin words in the Vulgate Bible based on the translation of Jerome in the fourth century CE. Evidently in the minds of the scholars who created the King James Bible, the word 'turban' was too strongly tied to the Ottoman Turks to describe biblical dress. It took more than four hundred years of non-biblical usage before

Artist unknown, *Lady Wrapping Her Turban*, 1675–1700, opaque watercolour and gold on paper, Andhra Pradesh, India.

'turban' was common enough to use in the New Revised Standard Version to describe clothes worn in the Old Testament. The edition of the Catholic Bible published in 1995 usually translates the vestment headdress as 'mitre', and reserves 'turban' for secular wear.

For the purposes of this book, the history of the wrapped turban begins in the Arabian Peninsula in the sixth and seventh centuries CE. Bedouins wrapped cloth into headdresses to protect themselves from intense heat. Other Arabian inhabitants lived in small cities, such as Mecca and Medina. Traders used camels to carry goods throughout the Fertile Crescent. They wore turbans and, with the emergence of an expansive Muslim religion, in two hundred years the wrapped turban spread from Arabia north to Turkish territory, east as far as the western border of the Indian subcontinent, and west across North Africa and into Spain.

The Qur'an, some forty chapters of revelation, came directly to the Prophet Muhammad from God. It is standard Muslim belief that the Prophet did not add his thoughts or feelings, and the Qur'an uses the word *ummi* to indicate that the Prophet was innocent of creating the text. This word is sometimes translated as 'illiterate', meaning that the Prophet lacked the ability to modify what he heard. The Qur'anic revelation came as voice, and the audience – the early Muslim community – wrote down what the Prophet recited.

The Qur'an prescribes veils for adolescent and adult women, but the scripture is largely silent on what men should wear. This includes the turban, *imamah* in Arabic, which was the standard headdress for Arab men. The first we read about the turban comes from hadiths, which are distinct from the Qur'an in that hadiths record the Prophet's own words or actions. A standard collection of hadiths registers that the Prophet prohibited pilgrims to Mecca from wearing turbans. That is, they must go through the rituals bareheaded. Other Hadiths record that the Prophet wore a black turban when paying an evening visit to his followers. In one of the Hadiths, the Prophet declares that the turban is the 'crown of the Arabs', and in another he states that 'the turban is the boundary between faith and infidelity.'[3] As the Muslim community expanded and came into often intense contact with non-Arabs in the Middle East, the turban signified a religious identity. What was once a geographical marker became a religious choice. Literary traditions other than the Hadith collections reflected a cosmopolitan culture. Popular among literate and illiterate Muslims were stories about the prophets of the Hebrew and Christian scriptures. In one story, Adam precedes his Edenic career as the ruler of paradise, wearing a crown. When he descends to Earth, he doffs the crown in favour of a turban.

Even though Arabs spread Islam into Spain and Sicily in the eighth century, their primary word for the turban, *imamah*, did not enter European languages. Rather, the word 'turban' comes from Safavid Iran. In Persian *dolband* means headband; the Indo-European word *band* is common to both the Persian and English words. As *dolband* made its journey through Turkish-speaking territory, it became *tulipan* and then entered Italian, Spanish and other European languages in different forms of 'turban', the 'L' and 'R' and 'P' and 'B' moving easily from one sound to the other. The word had its first English printing in Anthony Jenkinson's *Early Voyages and Travels to Russia and Persia* (1561): 'Upon his head was a tolipane with a sharpe end standing upwards halfe a yard long, of riche cloth of golde, wrapped about with a piece of India silke of twentie yards long, wrought with golde, and on the left side of his tolipane stood a plume of feathers.'[4] In the play *Cymbeline*, Shakespeare describes Muslims as 'impious Torbonds'. Even as late as Richard Burton's translation of the *Arabian Nights* in 1888, the word 'turband' was used instead of the current standardized 'turban'.

The turban and the tulip arrived in the West joined at the linguistic hip. When the tulip first arrived in Europe from the Ottoman Empire, nobody knew what to call this exotic flower. It was addressed with different names, from red lily to *lilionarcisus*, until its first written mention as *tulipan* in 1554 in conjunction with Augier Ghislain de

Busbecq. A Flemish herbalist and diplomat, Busbecq was sent as ambassador to the Porte or palace of the sultan in 1585. Legend has it that, while travelling among blooming tulip fields, he saw these flowers for the first time. He stopped to have a closer look and admire the blooms. Workers in the fields were wearing turbans, whose folds they decorated with tulips, and Busbecq pointed to the head of a worker, asking what it was. The interpreter answered 'tuliband', meaning the headdress and not the flower. The ambassador mistook the flower's name for the description his interpreter gave it, when he said the flower was like a tuliband in shape. Returning to France, he prepared his letters for publication (1589). In them he observed that 'we everywhere came across quantities of flowers – narcissi, hyacinths, and tulipans, as the Turks call them.' He also described the sultan's court as a 'sea of turbaned heads, each wrapped in twisted folds of whitest silk; look at all these marvellously handsome dresses of every kind and every colour . . . glittering with gold, with silver, with purple, with silk, and with velvet.'[5]

With some exceptions, such as the Sikhs, men usually shave their heads or close-cut their hair to wear a turban. They often wear some kind of cap, ranging from a close-fitting cap to a tall conical hat favoured by the Ottomans and Safavids in the fourteenth to nineteenth centuries. Shiite Safavid courtiers and urban elite wore a *taj*, a tall cap with twelve gores representing the twelve imams. The turban was wrapped in such a way that the top of the *taj* was visible. Throughout their history, Sufis generally wore a cap around which they wrapped low, rounded turbans. In the Muslim world, turbans may be taken off still wrapped – some homes have a 'turban chair' to this end – but customarily are unwrapped at doffing and rewrapped at donning. Elizabeth Taylor wore a sewn turban that she doffed and donned like a hat, whereas Las Vegas showgirls were locked into their lofty headgear with a strap below the chin.

The winding cloth usually measures at least 30 centimetres (12 in.) in width and the length varies between 3.5 and 9 metres (12–30 ft). All that fabric attests to the fact that a proper turban is not a single layer; it is not a bandana or headscarf. The long cloth is folded into smaller widths as it is wound about the head. The folding takes time and care, so wrapping the turban is an event. The longer the cloth, the more times it is folded and wrapped. In today's world, a Sikh may wrap 6 metres (20 ft) of cloth, daily spending 15–20 minutes getting a proper fit. To keep the turban in place, the wearer tucks the end of the cloth into one of the folds, sometimes leaving a tail hanging to the side or rear. Male Tuaregs in North Africa and Niger wear the *tagulmust*, a turban of cotton 4.5–6 metres (15–20 ft) long and 1 metre (3 ft) wide wound so that it covers the crown and the face except the eyes. They start wearing the *tagulmust* in adolescence and never appear in public without it for the rest of their lives.

The style of wrapping has always differed culturally and individually. Eighteenth-century jurists wore a conical lampshade; their theological colleagues wore the *urf*, a large spherical rolled turban. Safavid *Qizilbash*, elite warriors, wore white turbans made of twelve vertical padded folds ending in an upright baton-like finial. In the great Muslim empires stretching west–east from Constantinople to the Indian subcontinent and north–south from the Central Asian steppes to North Africa, fancy turbans were embroidered and decorated with tall feathers and single jewels or ropes of pearls. Most Sikhs today wrap the cloth in such a way that it forms a frontal peak.

Modest turbans are the colour of the natural fabric, usually cotton or linen, but many are dyed. In the Umayyad dynasty (seventh–eighth centuries), prayer leaders wore only white. In the succeeding Abbasid dynasty (eighth–thirteenth centuries), the caliph and court officials wore black turbans, symbolic of the Abbasids' rebellion against the Umayyads. The famous ruler Saladin rode into battle against the Crusaders wearing a black turban. In Mamluk Egypt (thirteenth–sixteenth centuries), the ruling Muslim Turks imposed sumptuary laws on Christians to wear white turbans and on Jews to wear yellow. Sixteenth-century Turkish descendants of the Prophet wore green,

Tuareg man wearing a white *tagulmust*.

as do today's Shiite clerics in Iraq and Iran, who claim descent from one of the holy imams. Today, many Arab Gulf men wear turbans, as do seminary students and teachers, prayer leaders and Sufi mystics throughout the Muslim world, including the diaspora.

In the West, the turban has been a fashion accessory on and off since the Renaissance, neither dominating any one fashion scene nor blotting out the headgear's religious origin. This is its allure. In the mid-eighteenth century Louis XV's mistress, the Marquise de Pompadour, dressed in public *à la turque*, including a turban, to amuse the king. Dolley Madison, the American First Lady who saved valuable papers and George Washington's portrait from the invading British in 1814, wore a turban as high (that is, European) fashion. Queen Victoria wore a dress-up turban as a child, and Abdul Karim, her personal attendant late in her reign, wore his conspicuously in court. The explorer Sir Richard Burton wore a turban when he disguised himself as an Afghan merchant while travelling through Arabia on a pilgrimage to Mecca. Back home recovering from a spear wound to his jaw, Sir Richard proudly wore a green turban as was his right as a hajji, one who had completed the pilgrimage (hajj). Alexander Gardner, one of many adventurers who sought their fortunes in eighteenth- and nineteenth-century India, went 'native'. He claimed he was a Scot even though he was born in the USA and lived only briefly in Scotland. The singular Gardner enjoyed fame in retirement in Kashmir as the 'Tartan Turban'.

In the contemporary Arabian Peninsula, home to Saudi Arabia and the smaller states on south and east coasts, many men wear a keffiyah rather than the more voluminous turban. The keffiyah is a single square cloth, usually made of cotton, bound to the head with a headband or head rope. This provides protection from the sun and generally covers the upper back and upper chest like a shawl. Sometimes the keffiyah is tucked up into the headband on the sides. T. E. Lawrence, popularly known as Lawrence of Arabia, broke with British military tradition by wearing a belted robe or skirt and keffiyah bound by a headband of two or three ropes. In the film version of Lawrence's adventure, made in 1962, the actor Omar Sharif, approaching from a long distance, rides into view through the shimmering heat of the desert, a keffiyah covering his head, neck and shoulders. The Palestinian leader Yasser Arafat always appeared in public in a tucked-up keffiyah. The cloth of the keffiyah may be chequered or plain. In most of the Peninsula, men who live in cities and towns removed from the desert life of the Bedouins still wear the Bedouin traditional headdress, and outside the Middle East it costumes young men and women sometimes as a statement of support for the Palestinian people.

The book will now follow the turban as it moves out of the Arab world into Europe, the Americas and West Africa. The next chapter starts the journey with the clash of Christian and Muslim armies in the Middle Ages and moves into the Renaissance, when artists placed turbans on biblical figures from the East, and royalty and aristocrats donned turbans for portraits and special events.

1

A Path into Western Iconography

By the eleventh century, many Christians in Europe had regular contact with Muslims and their turbans. Italian traders plied their commerce with the Mediterranean ports of the Middle East. Levantine Muslims served in Byzantine armies, and in Muslim Spain Christians lived side by side with large Muslim populations. Some Spanish Christians served in the Muslim regime's armies. But records of these routine interactions were deeply distorted by the bad press generated during the Crusades. With the exception of Saladin, texts and images describing the Crusades overwhelmingly portrayed Muslims as a threat to Christian civilization. Contemporary chronicles and poems, such as the *Songs of Geste,* ascribed to Muslims everything the Church found despicable. They labelled the Prophet Muhammad as the Church's arch-heretic. They claimed that Muslims worshipped a trinity of the Prophet Muhammad, Apollo and the god Tegavant; that in their mosques, they bowed before idols. In the early fourteenth-century *Divine Comedy,* Dante Alighieri put Saladin in limbo but consigned Muhammad (*Maometto*) to hell with his body split open. Muhammad was supposed to have been originally a Christian priest; because he promoted schism among Christians, he ended up mutilated by devils in the goriest of Dante's cantos (28).[1]

Images in manuscript illuminations, stone carvings and woodwork showed that medieval artisans had read about or heard of turbans. The standard term for Muslims was Saracens, and in European images they often wear *tortils,* headbands wrapped around a skullcap and tied on the side with a shoulder-length tail. A fourteenth-century illustration in William of Tyre's *Chronicle* imagines Saracens wearing *tortils*. Sometimes medieval images put a turban on the Saracen's head. A twelfth-century relic box shows a turbaned Saracen beheading the legendary St Valerie, who became famous for carrying her own severed head. In Madame Marie's *Book of Images,* two Saracens torture St Vincent; one of them wears a *tortil,* the other a turban. An illuminated thirteenth-century psalter places in the margin a turbaned Saracen threatening Christians in prayer in the text. Sometimes artists portrayed Saracens as grylluses, highly distorted humans or mixes of humans and animals. In the parish church of St Mary's in Adderbury, Oxfordshire, the underside of a pew seat, known as a misericord or mercy seat, is carved with a turbaned head on the two legs. A thirteenth-century English world map finds hermaphrodites wearing turbans inhabiting Egypt east of the Nile.[2]

Artists familiar with contemporary turbans placed them anachronistically on pre-Islamic events. A panel based on the Book of Judith in the *Arsenal Bible* (*c.* 1250) shows Holofernes consulting with his turbaned counsellors and then those counsellors bowing in fear after Judith decapitates the tyrant and holds his head aloft. Many Renaissance paintings depict Jesus's crowning with thorns. In Maarten van Heemskerck's version (*c.* 1550), a richly turbaned and bearded Jew looks out at the viewer and engages his attention. Manuscript illuminations placed turbaned onlookers at the Crucifixion, usually dark-skinned Saracens.[3] In *St Christopher Carrying the Infant Christ* (*c.* 1521) by Lucas van Leyden, a vigorous St Christopher, before his conversion to Christianity and not fully aware of the holiness of his passenger, carries the baby Jesus across a river. Christopher's carefully crafted turban with a jewel marks him as still unconverted.

Although Dante put the founder of the Muslim faith in hell, he put Saladin in limbo alongside Socrates and Plato. This was for his clemency towards Christian residents, when he successfully defended Jerusalem from the assault of Richard the Lionheart. There is no historical record that they encountered each other face-to-face or horse-to-horse, but a medieval chronicle records that Richard and Saladin not only met but duelled in combat. In an early thirteenth-century romance, Saladin challenges Richard to single combat and gives him a horse, which is a ruse. An angel warns Richard that the horse is but a colt that Saladin's dam is still nursing. Richard plugs the colt's ears so that it cannot hear its mother's neighing. Expecting Richard's mount to betray him, Saladin is unready for Richard's attack and falls in defeat. The fourteenth-century Luttrell Psalter illuminates this event, showing a dark-skinned Saladin wearing over his mail hood a large turban decorated with a seven-pointed peacock aigrette.[4]

Every year, Muslims from all over the world undertake the hajj, pilgrimage to the holy city of Mecca. They take the obligation as seriously as daily prayer and fasting during the month of Ramadan. In the fourteenth century Ibn Battuta, the son of an Islamic judge (*qadi*), not only travelled from Tangier across the North African Sahel to Mecca on a hajj but stayed in Mecca as a student for several years. He subsequently spent thirty years on the road, travelling as far east as China, as far west as Spain, as far north as Constantinople and as far south as East Africa. He was the most travelled man of the fourteenth century, logging more miles than Marco Polo.

When Ibn Battuta retired he wrote down his observations and adventures. In Alexandria, Egypt, he recorded that a judge wore the largest turban he had ever seen. For some Muslim officials, size mattered. In Damascus, he attended a debate between the conservative theologian Ibn Taymiyya and a rival from a different school of Islamic law. At issue was whether God descends from the heavens to the sky in the same manner that Ibn Taymiyya descends from the pulpit. When the rival disagreed, Ibn Taymiyya's supporters knocked off his turban, an essential marker of his status. For this breach of audience civility, the authorities arrested Ibn Taymiyya, who died while jailed.[5]

Although Ibn Battuta enjoyed a welcome and hospitality in most places he visited, when he was sailing from the Maldives to Java, European privateers attacked and took over the ship. They seized all his possessions, including his turbans and clothing. He and the other passengers made their way to Java, where the sultan provided him with 'three aprons, three undergarments, three middle clothing, three woollen mantles and three turbans' – enough for Ibn Battuta to continue his travels.[6]

Towards the end of his travels, Ibn Battuta visited Timbuktu, a centre of learning in Mali. The governor honoured his guest with robe, turban and trousers, all of dyed cloth. Ibn Battuta then sat on a shield, which the Malian chiefs lifted over their heads. Over the years he acquired so many robes and turbans in traditional welcoming ceremonies that several camels were required just to carry his wardrobe.

In 1433 Henry VI of England received an illuminated copy of John Lydgate's *Lives of Saints Edmund and Fremund*, which tells the story of an earlier invasion of Danish pagan warriors who killed Edmund, the king of Anglia. The king's cousin Fremund avenged Edmund's death, and founded a monastery in his honour. The illustrations in the manuscript presented to Henry VI show Danes in the garb of Eastern Muslims: tunics, scimitars and towering turbans. The artist transposed the dress of the Saracen enemies of the Crusaders to northern Europe, creating 'Viking Saracens'.[7] These images of turbans pre-date the first use of the word 'turban' by more than a century. The headdresses in the manuscript are elaborate and fantastic. One archer wears a beehive-shaped turban and another a pinkish turban crowned with rosettes. By the early 1400s, to the European the turban was a synecdoche for the Muslim and by extension all non-Christians, including the pagan Danes. In later manuscripts of Lydgate's *Lives* the turbans disappear.

The Ottomans emerged in the Central Asian steppes in the twelfth century. As they moved out of the steppes, they embraced Sunni Islam and turbans. Unlike other Turkish peoples, they were organized to rule a large territory, and unlike the armies of Genghis Khan and Timur, they did not conquer and fade away. In the twelfth century they moved into Anatolia and gradually expanded their territory until they crossed the Bosporus Straits and conquered the Byzantine capital, Constantinople, in 1453. Over the next two hundred years, the Ottomans steadily took over the eastern Mediterranean, Arabia and North Africa. At the same time, a series of wars with the Habsburg kings allowed the Ottomans to push north. At their peak, they controlled the Arab Middle East, North Africa and southeastern Europe, as well as Asia Minor. They brought a government, a disciplined army and navy, and the products of a literate elite: organized religion, books, architecture and painting.

As the Ottomans pushed north into Central Europe, European rulers and their courts looked upon them with understandable apprehension. But mixed with a dread of further loss of territory to the Turks was admiration for their military prowess and their commerce in Eastern silks and porcelains made in or coming through Turkish lands. Europeans were also fascinated by the Ottomans' court life. They excelled in courtly dress. Over plain undergarments, the sultan and his courtiers and high-level administrators wore two layers of robes, often embroidered, a belt and sash, and 6 metres (20 ft) of silk and cotton fabrics of different colours wrapped into turbans, often embellished with an aigrette.

The duchy of Burgundy in northeastern France, with its capital in Dijon, served as a pivotal cultural and political principality in the fourteenth and fifteenth centuries. By the mid-fifteenth century it had expanded into present-day Belgium and included the major cities of Ghent, Ypres and Bruges. Although officially subject to the French king, such dukes as Philip the Good ruled over an ethnically diverse realm, largely French- and Dutch-speaking, with strong ties to England. The prized textiles of Flanders used English wool.

Books of Hours set forth liturgical readings, such as the psalms, as well as prayers and hymns for daily devotionals. In the Middle Ages, before printing, they ranged from a petite 5 × 5 centimetres (2 × 2 in.) format to considerably larger sizes with illustrations. The courts of Europe commissioned the finest books for the elite. Among the most famous is the *Très Riches Heures*, commissioned by the Duc de Berry, a contemporary of Philip the Good. In this work, John the Fearless sits in profile, wearing a tall dark turban rolled to the front and festooned with a jewel. In the 1300s John joined the Nicopolis Crusade, which took him to Turkish Anatolia, where Sultan Bayezid I's army captured him. In captivity John took an interest in Turkish textiles and clothes, which he collected and, when ransomed from the Turks, brought back to Dijon. John was sufficiently enamoured of Turkish clothes that he dressed his son in Turkish pantaloons, shirts and turbans. John was sometimes known as John the Rash, for he inflamed the Hundred Years War (1337–1453) by murdering the Duke d'Orléans, Charles VI's younger brother. The ensuing French civil war – Burgundy was officially part of France – culminated when Orléans loyalists assassinated John.

By 1400, French manuscript illuminations commonly gave a variety of foreigners, both contemporary and historical, Turkish clothing. In the two years John the Fearless and three hundred knights awaited ransom, they collected artefacts and stories that they took back to a royal welcome in France. These contributions, plus the two-year visit of the Byzantine emperor and his entourage to Paris, gave French artists a better understanding of the variety of costumes in the East. Turbans became less generic. In an illustration in the prose and verse work *Chevalier Errant* (1394–6), 'Princes of the East' wear a variety of turbans found in the Islamic world. One wears an ellipsoidal turban with a large central gem, while another wears a turban wrapped around the lower part of a hat, giving the turban a brim. In the *Bible moralisée* (1402–3), an episodic Bible of moral instruction for French royalty, a scene of Jacob and Esau meeting after a long absence portrays Esau's retinue wearing a variety of exotic headdresses, including a turban of stacked concentric rings around a tall felt hat.[8]

Netherlandish Painter, *Man in a Turban*, *c.* 1440–50, oil on wood.

Meeting of the Wise Men; crowned kings Balthazar, Caspar and Melchior, each on horseback, from *Très Riches Heures du Duc de Berry*, 1420, tempera on vellum.

Robinet Testard – an illuminator and official court artist for Charles of Orléans, count of Angoulême, and his wife (later widow), Louise of Savoy, at the court in Cognac – painted many turbaned women in the late fifteenth and early sixteenth centuries. In his illustrations to an edition of Boccaccio's fourteenth-century *De claris mulieribus* (On Famous Women), he placed turbans on sixteen of his subjects. In the *Roman de la Rose*, Testard put turbans on Pygmalion's statue come to life, Venus embracing Adonis, and Lucretia being attacked by Tarquinius, giving them an aura of otherness. Some of Testard's women wear a white Abbasid or Mamluk turban with extensions descending the back. Others wear masses of braids plumped out below the turban and above the ears. Some wear a fuller and fatter Ottoman turban with a jewel or aigrette at the front. Sometimes turbans were satirized with other excessive headdresses, hennins and horn-shaped hats. Nevertheless, according to the historian John Block Friedman, the turban often ennobled its women: 'In his [Testard's] miniatures, such a headdress often conveys a positive and even ennobling significance to its female wearers.' Testard painted images with an eye sensitive to fashion, sometimes blending turbans with hairnets or snoods.[9]

These female turbans are varied and responded to contemporary fashion. Friedman analyses them as four main types: 1) simple, all white, wound, sometimes with a Mamluk 'flying' fabric down the back and sometimes folds of fabric coming below the chin; 2) a type in which masses of braids plumped out above the ears are separate from the rest of the turban, usually made of pieced panels; 3) studded with gems or feathers; 4) and a type in which braids instead of fabric are wound about the head, with a knot-like extension at the front, the whole forming either a bag around the head and hair or a snood for the side plaits, a style copied from Tarot cards.[10]

Numerous contemporary paintings featured turbans. A painting from 1410 of a lady by a Franco-Flemish artist shows her in profile, her fair complexion offset by a fur-lined collar, choker and embroidered dress below, and above by a jewelled rolled turban typical of the early fifteenth century's International Gothic style.[11] Figures in medieval religious paintings and sculptures are often silent likenesses of members of the ruling class. In the 1400s a noblewoman could have a portrait done of herself in the likeness of her name saint. The crusading king Louis IX brought Mary Magdalene's relics back from the Holy Land and placed them in an abbey that the dukes of Burgundy controlled. In Philip the Good's reign, a legend recorded that Mary Magdalene fled from Palestine and landed in Marseilles, where she converted the king and queen, then continued north to convert the pagan king and queen of Burgundy too. The portrait depicts a Burgundy princess posed in the guise of the Magdalene royally turbaned.

The painting depicts Margaret in contemporary style of dress with many pearls on her head and gown. Her turban of white silk shot with pale blue is studded with pearls on three bands of brocade with a trellis pattern. The turban is like Salome's in *The Martyrdom of St John the Baptist* (1510) from the St John Altarpiece. In this graphic painting the headless body of John the Baptist, arteries protruding from his neck, is placed in front of a Gothic arch. The executioner is garbed for his bloody work in a short cotton shirt, his loincloth tucked up, leaving his thighs naked. He places the severed head on Salome's tray. Salome is in a full-skirted dress and embroidered jacket, wearing a luxurious silk velvet turban. Her brocaded and bejewelled decoration is echoed in the decoration of her two armbands. She looks away demurely from her gory prize, untouched by the act of murder, merely presenting Herod with what she asked for. The turban marks her as hostile to the beloved John, yet it is part of her elegant outfit that denotes her as worthy of courtly life.

In the Gospel of Matthew (2:1–12), 'Magi', possibly astrologers from the East, see a star that they associate with the Jewish messiah. They follow it to Jerusalem and then Bethlehem, where they present gifts of gold, frankincense and myrrh to the baby Jesus. To avoid Herod's wrath, they return to the East by a route unknown to the Judean king. By the third century CE in Western Europe the Wise Men

Workshop of the Master of the Magdalen Legend, *The Magdalen*, c. 1510, oil on oak.

usually numbered three, corresponding to gifts for the Babe. By the Middle Ages, the three had names: Caspar, Melchior and Balthazar. They were not so much wisemen as kings who recognized Christ the heavenly king while he was still an infant. These kings were so central to celebrations of the Epiphany, which marked the recognition of the baby Jesus as Christ and heavenly king of the Christian Church, that European kings often chose 6 January as a coronation date. In the thirteenth century Africans, both freeborn and enslaved, were common enough in the ports of Italy that in literature and art black servants accompanied the Magi. In the 1400s the Roman church added Africa to the presumed reach of the Christian community, and Balthazar often took on the features of an African, sometimes wearing a turban.

Until the thirteenth century, the Magi wore Phrygian hats familiar to the ancient Greeks as an Anatolian headdress. With the arrival of the Turks, some European artists appropriated the exotic turban to add emotional depth to familiar classical and biblical scenes. Jacques Daret's *Adoration of the Magi* (*c.* 1434), part of a multi-panelled altar, features the third Magus, Balthazar, in a turban. He awaits his turn to present a gold vessel to the Holy Family, his elaborately rolled turban wrapped around his crown. He is an ancient and contemporary king, wearing both an ancient crown and a contemporary turban. In the panel, Joseph and Balthazar hold their right hands to their ears, listening for God's word. At Joseph's feet rests a flute. Daret gives each Magus a distinctive headdress. The second, Melchior, holds a fur-trimmed hat, and the kneeling Magus, Caspar, has placed his rustic

Jacques Daret, *Adoration of the Magi*, *c.* 1434, oil on wood.

hat on the ground. Daret has also given each a distinctive hairstyle: kneeling Caspar is bald; a feminized Melchior wears his hair long, neatly arranged down his back; while Balthazar has a scruffy head of hair and beard, an Asian holy man as well as a king.

In another panel painting, the *Presentation of Christ in the Temple* (*c.* 1434), Daret combines the Virgin's presentation of her son with her purification rite in the Jewish temple. Daret includes the Jewish prophetess Anna and her servant in an elaborate turban. The servant holds doves as a sacrificial offering for Mary's purification – for the birth, not the conception. This conformed to Catholic Church practice as well. Along with Simeon, who has been expecting the Messiah, Anna and her servant stand on one side of the altar across from Mary and Joseph. They are dressed expensively in contrast to Mary and Joseph, yet are bathed in light, evidencing their wonder at witnessing the presentation. The servant also carries a candle, which shines with the new revelation.

In the illustrated manuscript the *Heures d'Étienne Chevalier* (1452–60), a prayer of supplication to the mother of the Virgin Mary wears a large yellow turban. Here yellow signifies that Anne or Anna, the mother, is a Jew. The colour places her in a Jewish community in the Ottoman Empire; however, its size indicates her high status in the Christian community.[12]

Another early appearance of a turban-wearing Magus occurs in Rogier van der Weyden's St Columba altarpiece, completed in the mid-fifteenth century and now in the Alte Pinakothek in Munich. In the central panel, Caspar, the senior Magus, kneels before and touches the baby Jesus. Caspar's red hat sits at his feet. Balthazar waits his turn, holding aloft his white turban with its long tail. He is dressed in a beautiful embroidered tunic with a belt, from which his scimitar hangs. Further back in the queue of visitors, a bearded man with a white turban still on his head waits his turn.

Other examples abound. An anonymous contemporary Dutch panel, *The Adoration of the Magi*, also shows the third Magus with a turban wrapped around the base of a crown. An Austrian carved altarpiece dated 1406 shows Balthazar as an African wearing metal armour and a crown, and Melchior with a turban wrapped around his crown. Another anonymous contemporary Dutch panel of the Adoration of the Magi depicts both Melchior and Balthazar turbaned. Melchior holds a metal staff and wears an Ottoman fur-lined robe, while Balthazar's earring identifies him as African. In Andrea Schiavone's *Presentation of Christ* (1543–6), where turbans represent traditional authority, everyone wears them except Mary, Joseph and a Roman guard.

Dutch artists of the period appropriated the turban for several historical as well as biblical events. In a panel from 1500 by the Master of St Giles, St Rémy is converting an Arian bishop on the steps of Notre-Dame cathedral in Paris.[13] The Arian bishop wears a simple turban, alluding to Arius' home in Egypt in the third and fourth centuries and the Eastern flavour of his theology, which posited that Christ the Son was distinct from God the Father. Bernard van Orley went further in his *The Marriage of the Virgin* (*c.* 1513), National Gallery of Art in Washington, DC. Both female and male attendees wear turbans, but of different styles. One man's turban appears to be wrapped from ribbons, while the other's is wrapped around a pointed hat; the woman's turban rests on the back of her head and resembles an elaborate hairdo. These figures are not buried in the scene but are seen close up, the details of their garb highlighted. Several learned Jewish men in Orley's *Christ among the Doctors* of the same date, also in the National Gallery, wear turbans over skullcaps; the chief rabbi is accentuated by having a large white turban lifted high above his forehead.

The convention of marking Jewish authorities with turbans shows clearly in Dutch art. In *Burning of the Bones of St John the Baptist* (*c.* 1485), the Haarlem artist Geertgen tot Sint Jans depicted on the right side the Jewish authorities presiding over the cremation in high-crowned turbans; the Christian monks on the left, who rescue the bones, wear skullcaps.

Defendente Ferrari, *Adoration of the Magi*, *c.* 1520, oil on panel.

Joos van Cleve, *Black Magi*, of the triptych *Adoration of the Magi*, *c.* 1525, oil on oak panel.

An uncommon and prominent display of turbans appears in a central panel of a triptych from 1520 by an artist known as the Master of the Holy Blood. Wearing a conical turban, Pontius Pilate presents the scourged Jesus to a hostile crowd to decide his fate. Pilate's turban is pale pink and deeper pink in the folds. In the right panel, one of the crowd holds up his hands in dismay. He wears a red turban embellished with a central jewel.

Renaissance artists also used the turban as a signifier in historical paintings depicting classical scenes. From the *Histories* of Herodotus, Daret painted the death of Cyrus the Great, founder and ruler of the Achaemenid Empire in the sixth century BC. According to Herodotus, as Cyrus expanded his empire north from Persia, he threatened a kingdom ruled by Queen Tomyris. She vowed to kill him should he invade, and when he did, she carried out her threat. She trapped Cyrus and his army, had him beheaded and personally dipped his head in a vat of blood. In this scene, Daret dresses the queen and a servant in turbans, appropriating the contemporary Turkish turban to an ancient past. Consequent to Cyrus's death, the queen ruled what became the home of the biblical Magi.[14]

Even before the fall of Constantinople, tales of the Ottomans reached artists' studios. Early depictions of turbans on European men show distinctions in an era when headgear, arguably more than clothes, expressed personal fashion. Masaccio's *Young Man in a Turban* (1425–7) wears a bright red turban that is elliptical in form. The young man, shown in profile, has a studied look, perhaps barely breathing in order to keep the elaborately folded headgear in place. An early fifteenth-century illustration for Jean Froissart's fourteenth-century *Chronicles* shows several turbaned retinues of the French king Charles IV receiving a visit from his sister Isabella, wife of Edward II of England. Jan van Eyck's *Portrait of a Man* (1433) was a high point for this type of headgear depicted in the fashion capitals of Venice and Florence in the fifteenth and sixteenth centuries. A craggy middle-aged man with a two-day beard stares impassively at the viewer. His glowing red turban is an extravagance of folds and tucks, and it swirls upwards in luxurious fashion with the ends tied over his head. The painting may be the artist's self-portrait. In the Brukenthal National Museum in Sibiu, Romania, hangs the thematic companion piece, *Man with a Blue Turban* (*c.* 1433). This turban has draping that extends down either side of the sitter's face.

Jan van Eyck, *Portrait of a Man*, 1433, oil on oak.

Venice signed a trade agreement with the Ottomans in 1479. When the Turkish ambassador came to Venice, he noticed the Venetian painter Gentile Bellini at work. The ambassador returned to the Porte and spoke of Venetian art to Mehmed II, who decided to put himself firmly in the cadre of Western kings by obtaining a portrait by Bellini, running against the grain of an overall Muslim discomfort with images of humans. Bellini painted the sultan in profile as if through an arched window, suggesting the artist's distance from his royal subject. Mehmed was pleased and gave Bellini the title Palace Companion. The Bellini portrait was realistic and yet a declaration of the sitter's power. A contemporary reported that Bellini returned to Venice dressed *alla turca* in a turban and gold chain bestowed upon him by the sultan.[15]

Although the Habsburg court viewed the Ottomans as an infidel threat, other states, such as Florence and England, felt secure from an immediate threat and expressed by imitation their admiration for the Ottomans' military prowess. In 1510 Henry VIII and the Earl of Essex attended a Shrove Sunday festival dressed 'after the Turkish Fashion', for a bit of merrymaking before Lent.[16] A few years later the Midsummer Pageant featured a 'King of the Moors', dressed head to toe in Turkish finery.[17] At Shrovetide 1554 Queen Mary, Henry's daughter by Catherine of Aragon, hosted a masque in which the Turkish players wore turbans so large that they required internal frames of 'Asshen hoopewood' to hold their shapes. Henry's son by Jane Seymour, Edward, took part in a Masque of Young Moors in circa 1549. For the second Stuart king, Charles I, William Davenant produced the play *The Temple of Love*, in which India is represented by an 'Asiatique' riding on a camel and wearing a turban. Young nobles acting the part of Persian youths wore turbans 'silver'd underneath and wound about with white cypress and one fall of a white feather'.[18]

Sealing the fact that it referred to a somewhat familiar 'other', the turban was featured in the new genre of decorated maps. In the 1500s cartographers decorated maps with the Four Seasons or other

Gentile Bellini, *Sultan Mehmet II*, 1480, oil on canvas.

allegorical figures that projected their world view. Asia might wear a turban and flowing robes, carry an incense burner and have a camel at his side. (The imagery continued as late as a ubiquitous mid-twentieth-century Air France map.) In the sixteenth century German cartographers produced woodcut maps. They profited from improved surveying instruments. Johann Schöner, a Catholic priest who converted to the Protestant faith and became professor of mathematics at Nuremberg University, was a skilled map-maker. The art for the globe he made in 1515 came from an illustrated encyclopaedia, *Hortus sanitatis* (The Garden of Health). From the encyclopaedia's article on the orca, Schöner transferred to his globe an androgynous bearded mermaid/man with a sultry tail and complexly wrapped turban. The mythical sea creature symbolized the excitement of exploration in the same century that Christopher Columbus described seeing three mermaids before he landed in the New World.[19]

Before turning to the seventeenth century, let us give some thought to the term 'appropriation'. When European artists wanted to give a contemporary feel to their paintings of the Magi, they dressed them in turbans. That is, they appropriated them from another religious culture into their own. Some critics see this as a kind of theft, pulling from one context to another without permission. If the painters had portrayed the Magi as somehow belittling the Ottoman Turks, this kind of criticism would have validity. It would be insensitive to the feelings of the Turkish Muslims. But the turbans and their wearers in these paintings are anything but deprecating. Quite the opposite. The Magi are reverent before the Christ Child. They are dressed to the nines. Or it could be argued that the turbans are fanciful, anachronistic. Certainly, there is no biblical evidence that the Magi wore turbans. In fact, the Gospel of Matthew says nothing about their clothing, only their gifts. The appropriation is innocent of deceit or malevolence. The artists are celebrating an Eastern headdress, however fanciful.

2

Trade, Diplomacy and Depiction

In an expansion of trade with the East, the Dutch established the Amsterdam Exchange and the Dutch East India Company in 1602. The Exchange was situated on a canal with direct access to ships capable of sailing to Asia. Emanuel de Witte's 1653 painting of the Exchange includes a transaction among three men in the foreground. A turbaned gentleman in Ottoman or Persian dress approaches from the central square of the Exchange to enter a deal between a man, perhaps Armenian, in tunic and loose trousers, and an elderly gentleman in Dutch or northern European clothing in the centre.

To Peter Paul Rubens, the Antwerp-born artist of the Flemish Baroque, painting a Magus offered an opportunity to depict a personage wearing the height of luxury, a bird of paradise. In *The Adoration of the Magi* (1609), a throng of admirers presses down on the Holy Family. The Magi's attendants and their camels have borne gifts of gold and spices. Europeans with their horses look on. The Christ Child picks up a gold coin from Balthazar's offering. Rubens adorns the Black Magus's turban with an entire bird of paradise, head down, with full tail feathers and aigrette. This full-bodied bird carries strong associations with the valuable spices grown in the Moluccas (Spice Islands). The Dutch prized these birds, and the Dutch East India Company traded for them as well as for pepper, cloves, nutmeg and other spices from Southeast Asia.[1]

The bird of paradise figures in a later portrait of Prince Rupert, the son of Frederick v, king of Bohemia, and Elizabeth, the daughter of King James I of England. After a visit of the Persian ambassador Musa Beg to the Netherlands in 1625–6, Jan Lievens painted a portrait of Rupert in a blue turban embroidered with a bird of paradise. On Rupert's turban the bird is poised to take off as if on a foreign voyage. Diplomatic and trade relations between the Netherlands and Persia were strong enough that the Dutch painter Jan Lucasz. van Hasselt held the Safavid post of court painter from 1620 to 1629.

Dutch paintings record a range of turban styles designed in the artists' studios. The most famous portrait of a Dutch citizen in a turban is Johannes Vermeer's *Girl with a Pearl Earring* (*c.* 1665). Her turban is knotted on the top of her head and a tail of fabric falls straight down her back. Vermeer's studio props included a Turkish mantle, Turkish trousers and a black turban. Michiel Sweerts's subject in *Boy in a Turban Holding a Nosegay* (*c.* 1658–61) wears a neatly tied symmetrical wrap like a crown with the first, fringed band close to the

Shah Abbas II, engraving from Paul Rycaut, *The Present State of the Ottoman Empire* (1668).

Jan Lievens, *Boy in Cape and Turban (Prince Rupert of the Palatinate)*, *c.* 1631, oil on panel.

Jacob van Hasselt(?), *Wedding Dinner*, 1636, oil on canvas.

brow line. Rembrandt put a jaunty feather on an aged man's tightly wrapped turban in his *Bust of an Old Man with Turban* (1627/8). That feather places Rembrandt as borrowing from an eclectic closet of European attire stocked in the studios of various artists. Possibly the artist was influenced by the Persian dress of Musa Beg.

Rembrandt had a best friend and close contemporary in Lievens. Both were from middle-class families; Rembrandt's father was a miller and Lievens's an embroiderer. The two competed with and inspired each other, notably in their paintings and etchings of *The Raising of Lazarus* dated between 1630 and 1632. They even used the same man for a model of a villager, Rembrandt's surprised figure at the left and Lievens's leaning at the right of the scene. Rembrandt's interest in the theme might relate to mourning his father, who had died not long before. It also appears that Rembrandt altered one of his Lazarus etchings to create an *Entombment of Christ* for a series of Passion pictures. Lievens's image of Lazarus is set against a gloomy background, the

Rembrandt, *Man in a Turban*, 1632, oil on canvas.

burial cave. Contrastingly, Rembrandt shows a blinding light entering the scene through an opening in a heavy draped curtain as Christ raises his hand. The light causes Lazarus's accoutrements hanging against the curtain – a sword in its sheath, a bow and a turban – to glisten. The turban hangs with casual grace as if waiting to be traded with another artist or for Lazarus to take up his life again.[2]

Only a small fraction of the European public entered museums or studios where they could view portraits of turbaned men. Many more watched parades. During the visit of Mehmed IV's ambassador

Rembrandt, *The Raising of Lazarus*, *c.* 1632, etching and engraving.

to Vienna in 1665, crowds lined up daily to watch as his emissary Kara Mehmed Pasha paraded through the city with his band. Throughout the seventeenth and into the eighteenth centuries, Central European officials and aristocrats appeared at carnivals, weddings, coronations and baptisms dressed as Ottomans and accompanied by soldiers dressed up as Turks and by the musicians with which the Ottoman military was so strongly associated.

When in 1613 the 24-year-old Prince August of Saxony dressed as a sultan in a procession honouring the future elector's baptism, the presence of bearded and turbaned 'Turks' underscored his stature and pomp. European elites adopted the ceremonial function of the *mehter* (bandleader) and their armies started to employ its instruments and techniques, particularly in percussion, such as large Ottoman kettle-drums.[3] Similarly, when Prince Frederick August II married Maria Josepha of Austria in 1719, the gates of Dresden were gaily opened to Austrians costumed as Janissaries, a distinctively costumed Ottoman army regiment, and Italian acrobats sporting turbans in anticipation of the evening's entertainment.[4]

The cultivation of coffee beans flourished in Ethiopia from the fourteenth century. Trade to both the East and West was centred in Yemen, from where the beans were shipped eastwards to Persia and westwards to Constantinople. The Ottoman governor of Yemen introduced the drink to Suleiman the Magnificent (r. 1520–66). At the sultan's court the chief coffee maker (*kahvecibasi*) was chosen for his loyalty and ability to keep secret the method of roasting beans before brewing them. The *kahvecibasi* wore a loose shirt, trousers, colourful soft shoes and a white turban, a look distinct from the stiffer military gear worn by the powerful at court. Some illustrations show him grasping a pole with a coffee ewer suspended from it.

The scenery and costumes designed and produced in England by the architect and designer Inigo Jones in the first half of the seventeenth century put turbans on women as well as men. In Jones's notes for scenery and costumes for *Albion's Triumph*, he describes a a female

Joannes Meyssens after Cornelis Meyssens, *Sultan Mahomet (Mehmet) IV*, *c.* 1640–70, engraving.

captive wearing a plumed turban drawn to a peak behind; and another whose turban is covered by a scarf that went under her chin. *Britannia Triumphans* features a turbaned giant as well as a turban formed of crossed ribbons.

In the sixteenth century, coffee-houses in Constantinople became the venue for gentlemen to spend their leisure, conversing, listening to poetry and competing at backgammon. They were sometimes called *mekteb-i-irfan*, schools of learning, but the government closed them down, suspecting that habitués were neglecting their duties at the mosque. Moreover, conflict between Yemen and the Ottoman capital disrupted trade, encouraging Dutch and English merchants to ship coffee from Yemen to alternative markets in Europe. Coffee moved to Europe in dribs and drabs via emissaries and merchants. Some officials protested that the 'Islamic wine' was un-Christian, but in 1592 Pope Clement found the drink delicious – too delicious to leave to the infidels. He exclaimed, 'We shall cheat Satan by baptizing it.'[5]

Illustration from *Two Broad-sides Against Tobacco* (1672).

Shops that served coffee brought a new social habit to Europe's intellectual life. The first English coffee-house, the Angel, was opened in 1650 by a Turkish Jew in Oxford. Others followed. Gatherings at the coffee-house at any time of day gained popularity with university students and faculty, one group of which created the embryo of the Royal Society, members of which include illustrious names in the history of modern science, such as Francis Bacon and Isaac Newton. The latter once dissected a dolphin on the long table of the Grecian Coffeehouse, founded in London in 1665.

Pasqua Rosée, possibly a Greek from Sicily, who already had established coffee-houses in Oxford and Paris, opened London's first in 1652. Today its location is marked with a wooden sign in the shape of Rosée's head. Merchants patronized London coffee-houses, which came to be called 'penny universities' because men for the price of a coffee could get out of the home and gather in them to read newspapers and share opinions. At the time, the Ottomans were advancing on Vienna, but the Austro-Hungarian Empire was distant and the 'Turk's head' signs on shops spelled welcome, not an infidel threat. A contemporary poem about the coffee-house emphasized its Turkish character:

> To view the Potts or Broom flick where
> The Signs of Liquours hanged are.
> And if you see the great Morat
> With Shash on's head instead of hat,
> Or any Sultan in his dress . . .
> Of if you see a Coffee-cup
> Fil'd from a Turkish pot, hung up
> Within the clouds, and its Pipes,
> Wax Candles, Stoppers, these are types and certain signs
> (with many more
> Would be too long to write them 'ore,)
> Which plainly do Spectators tell
> That in that house they Coffee sell.[6]

The historian Bryant Lillywhite tallied the number of coffee-houses imitating Rosée's sign of a Turk's head in London as fifty between 1652 and 1900.[7]

Coffee-house token with image of Sultan Murat on obverse, 1648–73.

The trajectory of the East African drink in France was more of a top-down phenomenon. Suleiman Aga, the Turkish envoy to the court of Louis XIV, brought a quantity of coffee not only for himself but for his retinue. Enterprising Middle Eastern merchants created a party atmosphere around coffee, which became all the rage. A description by Isaac D'Israeli (father of Benjamin) in *The Curiosities of Literature* (1791–1823) attests that enslaved black servers were part of the exoticism:

> On bended knee, the black slaves of the Ambassador, arrayed in the most gorgeous Oriental costumes, served the choisest Mocha coffee in tiny cups of egg-shell porcelain, hot, strong, and fragrant, poured out in saucers of gold and silver, placed on embroidered silk doylies, fringed with gold bullion, to the grand dames, who fluttered their fans with many grimaces, bending their piquant faces – be-rouged, be-powdered, and be-patched – over the new and steaming beverage.[8]

Parisians drank it with only a small measure of sugar until another coffee drink, cappuccino, was introduced from Hapsburg Vienna. The first commercial cafés were tented affairs, such as the Foire Saint-Germain, where women as well as men were welcomed by hosts in flamboyant robes, pointed slippers and turbans. As the vogue developed, street sellers, garbed in at least the rudiments of costume, circulated in Paris bearing coffee in large jugs heated by portable lamps.

If the English coffee-houses were typically oak- or hickory-panelled, early French ones were furnished with carpets and marble tables, aglitter with candlesticks and candelabra. And whereas the British cafés were clubby, and having a token with an emblazoned sultan in one's pocket meant belonging to a cadre of society, at the French cafés customers provided a spectacle. Appropriate to the glamour of the coffee emporiums, François Procope opened the Café Procope directly opposite the Comédie-Française theatre. Philosophers, dictionary-makers and revolutionaries met to converse and debate in the cafés. Napoleon Bonaparte played chess in the de la Régence while still a common artillery officer.

The international dynamics of royalty intermarrying across the map of Europe was a competition backed by royal spectacles and extravagant clothes. In 1572 the future Henry IV wed Marguerite de Valois in the cathedral of Notre-Dame, Paris. Princes wore jackets of pale yellow satin covered with raised embroidery and ornamented with pearls and gems. Ladies were brilliant in brocade and cloth-of-gold velvet brocaded in gold and laced with silver, and Marguerite wore a crown and a speckled ermine belt; on her shoulders was a large blue mantle with a train 3.5 metres (4 yd) long. The king and his nobles wore turbans and Turkish costumes at the masquerade ball. Allegorical entertainment and a tournament lasted for four days, but beneath the grand display were anger and hostility, evidenced by how the Catholics were ornamented and the Protestants underdressed.

The lavish Renaissance masquerades of England and France evolved from Italian carnival celebrations in the 1500s. A courtly masquerade was one of François I's political tools when he sought an alliance with Suleiman the Magnificent. A French regent, whether Catherine de' Medici, François I or Louis XIV, ruled over the choice of costumes, which were coordinated like the music and dance. Catherine de' Medici dazzled all Europe with her vast costume parties, but there were bevies of pretend river gods and sirens, not foreigners. In 1662 a grand masque at the French court proclaimed the glory of Louis XIV, the Sun King. A theme of Turquerie (the Western fascination with and imitation of aspects of Turkish culture) was used to serious purpose. Along the lines of the English masques beloved of Queen Anne, the pageant paid allegorical homage to a monarch. Performers represented different continents – Europe, Asia and America – thus parallel to the maps that had the bearded Asia. In the first quadrille, Louis, costumed as a Roman emperor, carried a device of the sun. In the second, Louis's brother Philippe (Duke of Orléans), dressed as the king of Persia, carried a moon. The Prince de Condé led the third quadrille as emperor of the Turks. His motto was *Crescit ut Aspicitur* (He prospers as he is favourably regarded). The prince rivalled the king in the splendour of his costume and the improbability of his turban. The historian Julia Landweber describes it:

> He wore a costume of silver-embroidered red satin, liberally strewn with diamonds and turquoises, and, to emphasize his Turkish character, both he and members of his quadrille hung silver crescents from every angle of their bodies: calves, elbows, backsides, shields, turbans, and horses' saddles all featured the Muslim crescents in shimmering loops and flying chains.[9]

The slant of detailed illustrations of Charles Perrault's masquerade was many nations. The Prince de Condé is shown in periwinkle-blue, navy and white. His turban is formed of layers of silver jewel work, surrounded by brocade, its bands overlaid with silver and garnished with diamonds and turquoise. Each figure in the illustrations is both elegant and fanciful. Seven years after this masque, Hugues de Lionne, Louis XIV's minister for foreign affairs, appeared costumed as France's 'grand vizier' for an audience with Suleiman Aga.

Diplomatic exchanges and accounts of voyages fed the fashion of Turquerie during the Rococo period. Outstanding among English scholar-travellers, Paul Rycaut rode the crest of the Orientalist wave thanks to his years in Constantinople and Izmir. He first travelled as secretary to the British ambassador to the Ottoman court in 1660. In the same year he published *The Present State of the Ottoman Empire*, which contained 29 engravings, some with turbans, recording how military and administrative officers at the Porte dressed. *Mahometes Quartus* (Mehmed IV) is the only bust portrait in Rycaut's iconic

Illustration depicting a timbal and trumpet player in Charles Perrault, *Courses de Testes et de Bagues Faittes par Roy et par les Princes et Seigneurs de sa Cour, en l'année 1662.*

work. Folds create a solid and circular turban, into which are pinned bristles like upside-down paintbrushes used to drape chains of jewellery. Pages and attendants as well as Janissaries and chief functionaries wear particular headgear, from peaked cones to bulbous turbans. Rycaut illustrated deaf mutes and dwarfs, the former reputedly with a superior ability to keep secrets, the latter known as witty entertainers. In one illustration, a high-placed black eunuch wears a turban that flies upwards like the sail of a ship. Rycaut believed his monograph would educate his countrymen on the costume of the Turks, as well as providing entertainment, hence the specificity:

French School, *Enjoying Coffee*, first half of the 18th century, oil on canvas.

When he is set upon the Bench all causes are brought before the *Caddeelescheer* who is Lord Chief Justice, and by him all judgements pass unless the Prime Visier shall think the cause proper for his cognizance, or shall disapprove at any time the sentence of the judge; and then by virtue of his unlimited power he can reverse the Verdict and determine as he pleases. All Officers in the Divan wear

> a strange sort of dress upon their heads . . . which for the most lively description is here delineated before you.[10]

One turban is illustrated all by itself. Labelled 'A Turbant', the picture shows a tall melon-shaped turban with a topknot. The twisted fabric either hung down like a braid of hair or was swept up (as in the picture). Rycaut's book was quickly translated into several languages. A year after its original publication in English in 1660 it appeared in French. Louis XIV may have seen the volume as he was assigning Molière to write *Le Bourgeois gentilhomme* (The Middle-Class Gentleman), which premiered in 1670.

The visit of Suleiman Aga to the court of Louis XIV in 1669 is most remembered for its problems with protocol. His first formal audience was with Lionne, in Suresnes (not Versailles). Lionne wasn't apprised of Suleiman's rank, as the *lettre de créance* of his credentials was to be delivered only to the king. But Suleiman had another letter addressed to the Grand Vizier of France, so Lionne decided to dress up as a Turkish grand vizier and receive the diplomatic mission in elegant Turkish attire. This seemed to solve the quandary of whether he was a diplomat of highest rank. He did the interview dressed in a black robe, a Christian cross hanging on a blue ribbon on his chest and sitting on a carpet with brocade cushions.

Turks appeared on stage as well as within picture frames. It fell out as follows. Laurent d'Arvieux, a merchant and linguist who may have been a secret agent of Louis XIV, wrote his travel memoirs of much of the Middle East, especially Turkey. In an engraving he looks comfortable on a Rococo settee, wearing a silk suit and powdered wig. However, Chevalier d'Arvieux understood the cultural sensitivities of the Ottoman embassy and arranged for his 'Turkish and Arabian clothes' to be brought from Marseilles so that he could wear them when Suleiman met the king himself. D'Arvieux recorded in his memoir that Louis XIV's mistresses Madame de Montespan and Madame de Vallière detained him for several hours for his sartorial help, keen to be sure they looked and behaved as Turkish ladies would: 'At the end of dinner the King went into his study . . . and I entertained the two ladies with an account of the details of a Turkish marriage.'[11]

Louis XIV made sure that he was in his most opulent guise for the audience with Suleiman when at last the latter reached Versailles. The king dressed in gold brocade studded all over with diamonds. Since the diamonds were from Western Asia, they conveyed to the ambassador the reach of France's power. An engraving avers that the finely dressed, turbaned Turks did not wear sabres or armour to the king's audience.

A comedy of errors occurred when Suleiman and the king met face to face. The French royal translator could read Turkish but not

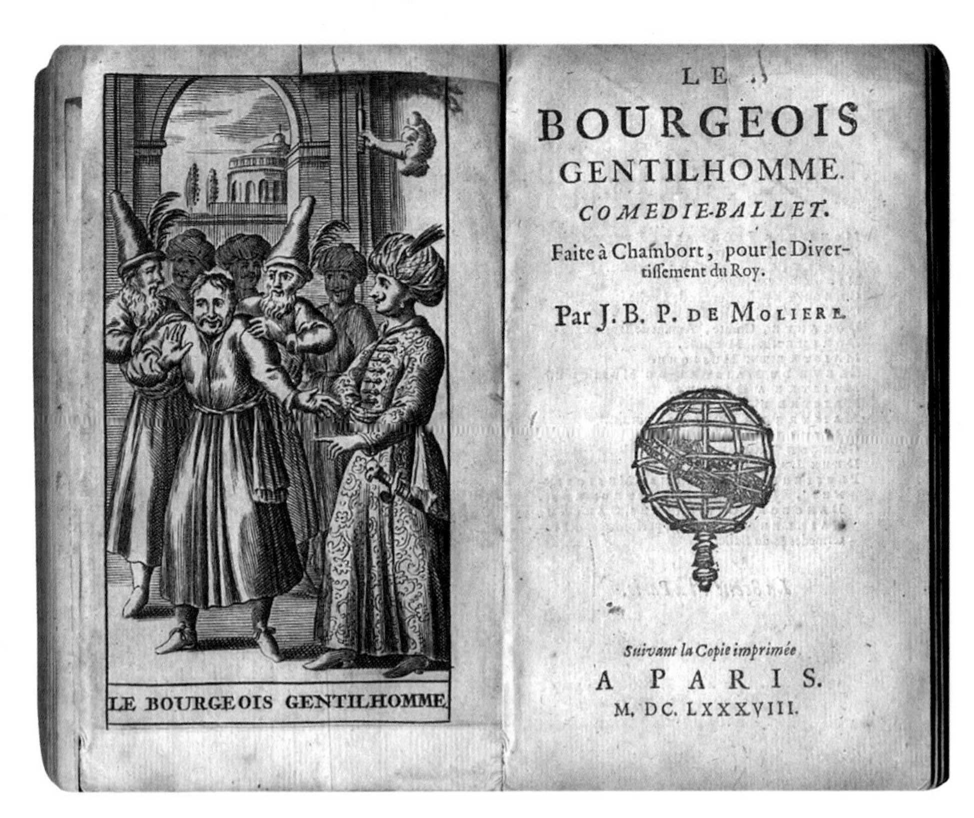

LE BOURGEOIS GENTILHOMME.

COMEDIE-BALLET.

Faite à Chambort, pour le Divertissement du Roy.

Par J. B. P. DE MOLIERE.

Suivant la Copie imprimée

A PARIS.

M. DC. LXXXVIII.

Molière, *Le Bourgeois gentilhomme* (1688 edn).

speak it, and besides had left his Turkish dictionary in Paris. This inspired a commission from the king to Molière to write *Le Bourgeois gentilhomme*. One can only be grateful to the Sun King for having momentarily lapsed into humour. The play became the most performed in French history, inspiring costumers to spoof what a pretend Turk might wear.

Having had the etiquette of encounter smoothed out, Louis XIV commanded Molière to work with the court musician, Jean-Baptiste Lully, for a ballet within the play, and with d'Arvieux to ensure the authenticity of Turkish customs and garb. The play with a ballet suite was first performed at Chambord in October 1670 in the Théâtre de Palais-Royal and for the public in November. The leitmotif of the merchant M. Jourdain who tries to be an aristocrat by consorting with pretend Turks starts and ends the play. His wife and servants are sensible people who try to draw him back to reality, whereas a pair of minor aristocrats trick him into giving them money.

Sporting gentlemanly clothes was a means of rising in social class that Jourdain took to comic lengths, just like the fairy tale 'Puss in Boots', which was published less than two decades later. In the final act, Mme Jourdain says her husband is dressed for a masquerade, but he replies that this is the morning robe of a *gens de qualité* (person of quality). He tells her that he is a *Mamamouchi*, a chevalier, a status he has achieved through a ceremony called a *Mahometa-per-Jordina*. More gibberish follows. Although he longs to be accepted at the king's court he can find only one means to infiltrate it: by having his daughter Lucille marry the son of the Grand Turk, in actuality a boy of his own (middle) class, Cleondis, whom his daughter loves. In the gibberish, one makes out '*da turbanta*'.

In *Orientalism in French Classical Drama* (2002), Michèle Longino points to the 'carefully orchestrated performance of mimicry, mockery, and menace' in the comedy and identifies it as pre-colonial: 'If we do not have colonialism here, we have all the markers of the will to colonize.' She writes,

> Molière's play was not merely a comedy with a few 'Turqueries', but a compensatory exercise in which the French indulged to console themselves for their inability to manage the Ottomans to their advantage and to keep the French nouveaux riches in their place. What they couldn't control in the world, they would control on the stage . . . If Louis XIV and his court were seeking to get the upper hand and have the last word on a situation that threatened to elude them, the evidence is, to the contrary, that the situation had already gotten the best of them. That they had to stage this play for themselves suggests to what extent the Ottoman world (with no deliberate intent), as well as the local bourgeois (with considerably more), had actually succeeded in colonizing the French aristocratic imagination.[12]

The turban of M. Jourdain must be imagined, but it was surely part of the protagonist's outfit. The play's fame at court and in Paris amplified the cultural influence of Suleiman's visit, and there is testimony from Rycaut that the novelty of Turkish dress, specifically the white turban, appealed to 'common people':

> It is no small inducement to the common people, who is most commonly won with outward allurements, to become Turks; that when they are so, but a white Turbant . . . we shall not wonder if the ignorant and vain amongst Christians . . . should be catched and entrapt with the fancy and enticement of the Turkish Mode . . . and thus the Turk makes his habit [clothing] a bait to draw some to his superstition.[13]

Shakespeare wrote *Othello* in the early 1600s. The Ottomans, despite losing the naval battle at Lepanto in 1571, were steadily overrunning Habsburg territory in Eastern Europe. Barbary pirates from North Africa routinely captured English ships and enslaved their crews and passengers, who 'turned Turk' to save their lives. Othello, the military commander and 'Noble Moor', has a dark, probably Muslim past that he cannot fully shake. He defends Cyprus from the Turks and elopes with and marries Desdemona, daughter of a Venetian senator. Yet he turns Turk in swallowing the lies of his comrade Iago, who claims Desdemona's adultery. In a rage, Othello smothers his wife, then discovers the truth about her innocence. In his final speech at her deathbed, he states,

> in Aleppo once
> Where a malignant and a turbaned Turk
> Beat a Venetian and traduced the state,
> I took by th'throat the circumcised dog
> And smote him thus. (v.2)

Othello in one breath defends his status as a Venetian by recounting how he slew a Turk who had assaulted a Venetian in Aleppo, and in his next breath turns the dagger on himself, the murderer of his beloved wife. Just as he once murdered another for violating a Venetian, he now slays himself, an act of circumcision that separates him from the Christian and innocent woman. Paintings of Othello often feature the military leader wearing a turban, but in the play a turban is only mentioned being worn by a single person, the unnamed Turk whom Othello killed. We can safely say that in costume, Othello is Venetian. In the second marker of a Muslim man, circumcision, Othello regressed to his dark, Muslim past in the broad stroke of his dagger.

Although Shakespeare ridiculed the by now clichéd 'Turk play' in *Henry IV, Part 2*, audiences by 1600 were not surfeit. In the Jacobean dramatist Robert Daborne's *A Christian Turn'd Turke; or, The Tragical Lives and Deaths of the Two Famous Pirates Ward and Dansiker* (1612), one of the pirates converts to 'Mahomestism' and a mufti, an Islamic scholar of religious law, places on his bare head a turban and girts him with a sword. Two decades prior, the sultan of Turkey had appeared in Christopher Marlowe's *Tamburlaine the Great* (1590) as a grand monarch and global power. A wide-sleeved robe, slippers and exotic headgear signalled to an Elizabethan audience that a character was from a remote and little-known part of the world. The costume had an inherent staginess, potent enough that spectators in the back row of the theatre could recognize the trope. Süheyla Artemel has analysed the imagery and themes of the Turk in Elizabethan and Jacobean drama of this era. She suggests how stage properties connected with Turks were used for dramatic effect:

> The Turkish banners ('moony standards'), the turbans, the statue or brazen head representing the supposedly Moslem idol, 'Mahomet', 'Turkey clothes', the mustachios curled up 'the Turky waye', the falchion or the scimitar and the Turkish bows and arrows, are items to which countless allusions are made, both in the actual text of a play as well as in the inventories of stage property . . . The 'turban'd Turk' with his black moustache, his Oriental costume, and his scimitar, was a colourful figure of the drama; as an image he evoked a wealth of emotive and intellectual associations that bear testimony to the imaginative vision and the mental awareness of the Elizabethan dramatist as well as his audience.[14]

In the Ottoman Empire, a farrago of many ethnic and religious communities, the turban had a strong Islamic identity. A dramatic example of this involved the messianic career of Sabbatai Zevi (1626–1676), a Sephardic Jew from Smyrna in southwestern Anatolia, whose claims included returning Jews to Israel, their Promised Land. Sabbatai inspired a large following extending south to Egypt and north and west to major European cities. Unsettled by reports that he planned to overthrow the sultanate, the Ottomans imprisoned him, but his following continued to expand. Finally, court officials gave the messianic claimant the choice between a painful death and conversion to Islam. To the dismay of many of his followers, he signalled the conversion by donning a turban, easily available in Muslim Turkey but forbidden to Jews. Others remained steadfast, arguing that the 'evil clothing' on his head did not signify that he was no longer 'like the body of Heaven in his purity'.[15] Sabbatai proved an inconstant Muslim, interspersing his messianic claims with outward conformance to Islam. Eventually, Ottoman officials banished him to Greece, where he died. However, a small community of Jewish converts to Islam endured and even flourished into the twentieth century, when the revolutionary Young Turks restricted turban-wearing to Muslim clergy.

Sir Anthony van Dyck, *Sir Robert Shirley*, 1622, oil on canvas.

3

Nabobs, Adventurers and Travellers

The Ottoman Turks and Safavid Persians were arch-rivals. Often they warred against each other. Yet throughout their rivalry they exchanged gifts, as European royalty did. The exchange of gifts included fine clothing and textiles as well as camels, falcons and illustrated and bejewelled books. Gift-giving sometimes smoothed their political relations. In 1522 the Persian ambassador Ali Quli Agha arrived at the enthronement of the sultan with a retinue of 120 men wearing gilded turbans, followed by another 200 men on horseback in gold-embroidered robes, as well as hundreds of merchants and several thousand servants on camels, donkeys and horses, bearing gifts for the new sultan.

At other times, gifts punctuated their rivalry. Before the Battle of Chaldiran in 1514, on the verge of war, the emperors challenged each other's potency with gifts. Selim sent to Ismail a handkerchief of the type worn by Persian women, exposing his impotence. In an accompanying note, Selim wrote: 'For you, who is unworthy to be called a man, these are more fitting than a turban and a helmet.'[1] On another occasion he sent Ismail a set of Sufi attire, because, as the accompanying letter stated, 'You are from a line of Sufis' and, by implication, unfit to govern. Shah Ismail responded by dispatching Quli Agha with a golden casket stamped with the royal seal and filled with a drug for the use of the Ottoman scribes, implying that they must have been under the influence of drugs to write such a nasty letter. Ismail's gift hit a nerve, and Selim ordered the messenger executed on the spot.[2]

Anthony and Robert Shirley were among the earliest English travellers to Persia who interacted with the shah. Anthony, who traded successfully in Venice in the late sixteenth century, took it upon himself to sail to Persia, both to establish 'commercial intercourse' with England by shipping Persian carpets and textiles through a southern port, and to ally England and Safavid Persia against the growing power of the Ottoman Turks.[3] Eventually he trained thousands of horses for the shah's army.

Robert joined Anthony in Persia in 1598. Although the brothers were not able to negotiate secure trade routes between the two countries, Robert remained there for most of his life, marrying a Persian Christian and dressing according to the fashions of the royal court. His status at court was such that Shah Abbas assumed the responsibilities of godfather to one of his children. In 1609 Robert, a devout Catholic, arrived in Rome dressed as a Persian but with his turban surmounted by a gold crucifix to show his faith. He removed his turban to kiss the feet of the pope, then devoted his audience to urging for a union of Christian rulers against the Turks. Two years later Robert represented Shah Abbas at the court of James I. Again, he dressed in Safavid style, including a notable turban, which presented the problem of whether he would remove his headgear in the presence of the king. A compromise entailed removing his turban, laying it at the king's feet, then putting it on again.[4] Acting as an emissary of the English Crown, Robert sailed to India, visited the Mughal court and returned to Isfahan with two elephants.

In 1622 Robert again visited Rome, where Anthony van Dyck painted his portrait. He wore a gold tunic lavishly decorated with human figures and flowers over a gold and silver robe highlighted by orange bows down the front, doubtless made by court tailors in Isfahan. His Safavid-style turban was wrapped in many folds with orange highlights, which picked up the bows of his robe. Adorned with an aigrette, the turban's volume is much larger than Robert's head. A contemporary churchman, Thomas Fuller, observed that Shirley 'much affected to appear in foreign vests, and as if his clothes were his limbs, accounted himself never ready till he had something of the Persian habit about him'.[5] The death of James I in 1625 ended Robert's status as ambassador. The British East India Company commissioned a Persian as the shah's representative, and when Robert sailed back to Persia, he had lost access to the court. He died in Persia, where he was buried. An inventory of his possessions listed 'horses, camels, vests, turbans, and a rich Persian dagger'.[6]

The Mughals, another Turkish people, took over the Indian subcontinent in the sixteenth century and ruled most of it until the British deposed the last emperor in 1857. The Mughal Empire embraced Persian language and culture, Shia as well as Sunni Muslims, and Hindu Rajputs. Emperor Akbar promoted an ecumenical policy of tolerance of religious diversity. The Mughals were justly proud of their architecture, the most famous building being the Taj Mahal in Agra, south of Delhi. The Mughals hosted the British East India Company, which gave significant numbers of Britons their first encounters with turbans on live people.

Queen Elizabeth I had established the British East India Company in 1600 to compete with the Dutch and Portuguese for sea routes carrying spices to the West. When the British abandoned their colonial enterprise in North America, they doubled down in South Asia. By 1800 the East India Company controlled Bengal in eastern India, and most of central and southern India. Trade flourished, mostly in the export of spices, cotton and silk to Britain, and officials of the Company grew wealthy and desirous of lasting records of their lives in India.

In 1634 the writer and traveller Henry Blount took an eleven-month journey through the Ottoman Empire. He dressed as a local on his tours not out of an inclination to adopt a new persona, but for safety. In his *Voyage into the Levant* (1636), he advises: 'If you wear a turban, you must of necessity shave your head. As for the beard, they never mind them in Turquie, the greatest being accounted the handsomest.'[7] From a distance, his caravan of horses and their riders looked pretty much like any Turkish, Persian or Arab entourage. On one occasion, bandits did accost Blount's party, but his Turkish garb persuaded the bandits to settle for loot rather than lives.

Captain James Cook stretched British naval prowess into the far Pacific. He brought back to Britain the words 'taboo' and 'tattoo'

Arthur William Devis, *Portrait of a Gentleman*, c. 1785, oil on canvas.

(Polynesian *tapu* and *tatau*) and a variety of Polynesians as guests. Among these visitors was Omai, a prince in search of arms to re-establish himself on the island of Ra'iatea, from which he had been exiled. In 1774–5 George III and British high society celebrated Omai as an exotic figure from the far reaches of the expanding British Empire. Joshua Reynolds painted Omai enveloped in a heavy robe, long sashes and a full white turban with a long tail hanging down the right side of his head. His left hand is fully tattooed and his feet are bare. He was certainly the first and possibly the only tattooed and barefoot prince to pose in a turban.[8]

Reynolds and the Anglo-American artist John Singleton Copley (see Chapter Four) flourished in Georgian England, but most artists struggled to make a living with brushes and paint. Many wealthy aristocrats travelled to Italy for portraits or cityscapes to bring home. Royalty and others invited Dutch artists to England to capture on canvas portraits of individuals and families. Some English and Scottish artists sailed east as a career move. Tilly Kettle was one of the first to land in India. In 1772 he painted Antoine Polier, a French Swiss engineer in the employ of the nawab of Oudh. Like a number of Europeans working in India, Polier embraced local dress. Kettle's portrait presents him reclining before three nautches (dancing girls). He wears a long *jama* or full-length shirt, an embroidered jacket and a turban. (The Urdu word *jama* entered English as 'pyjama', something comfortable to wear around the house.) Kettle painted many portraits during his years in India, and a number of his paintings were displayed in London when he returned to continue his career there. His success encouraged other artists to follow suit.[9]

A contemporary, George Willison, painted Nancy Parsons (Anne, Viscountess Maynard) in Turkish attire in about 1771, before he left England for India. Parsons had affairs with numerous aristocrats, including the Earl of Shelburne and Richard Rigby, a Privy Councillor. In Willison's portrait, she wears a white silk robe and a black satin turban. Next to her on the settee lies a basket of yarn that she has been knitting with. Willison also painted the turbaned nawab of Arcot, a principality just inland from Madras, and sent it to the British king, George III.

Unlike Willison, who returned to England after six years in India, Thomas Hickey came to stay. He painted many notable Kolkatans, including Frances 'Begum' Johnson, the queen of Calcutta society, and Indian nawabs in a variety of turbans. David Ochterlony was one of many Britons who adopted an Indian lifestyle. Born in Boston, Massachusetts, as a young man he fled the American colonies in revolt and, via Canada, arrived in England, where he entered the British East India Company's army in 1777. Through his connection with William Kirkpatrick, a major-general in the Company's army, he rose steadily to the rank of general, amassed a great fortune, cohabited with several Indian women (*bibis*) and adopted Indian dress wholeheartedly.

A drawing by Charles D'Oyly in *The Costume and Customs of Modern India* (1813) shows a British gentleman in his bedroom in India at the outset of his day. Four turbaned African bearers attend him. The enslaved house servants wore turbans during a range of activities from secretarial duties to cooking to making the bed. In the drawing, one stands and reads a missive aloud. Another has pushed the gentleman's long striped cotton robe up over his knees and feet, and another at a distance prepares a repast. The fourth makes his bed by hanging the mosquito netting. For the colonial British it seems to have been an idyllic existence.

In 1970 U.S. Vice President Spiro Agnew attacked those critical of President Richard Nixon's Vietnam policies as 'nattering nabobs of negativism'. At no loss for alliteration, he followed this by 'hopeless, hysterical hypochondriacs of history'. All the words were easy to understand except 'nabob', which certainly sent some newspaper readers and television viewers to their dictionaries. The word entered English from India, from the Urdu *nawab*, a deputy appointed to rule a region of the Mughal Empire. In English parlance, nabobs were employees of the British East India Company, some of whom prospered in India.

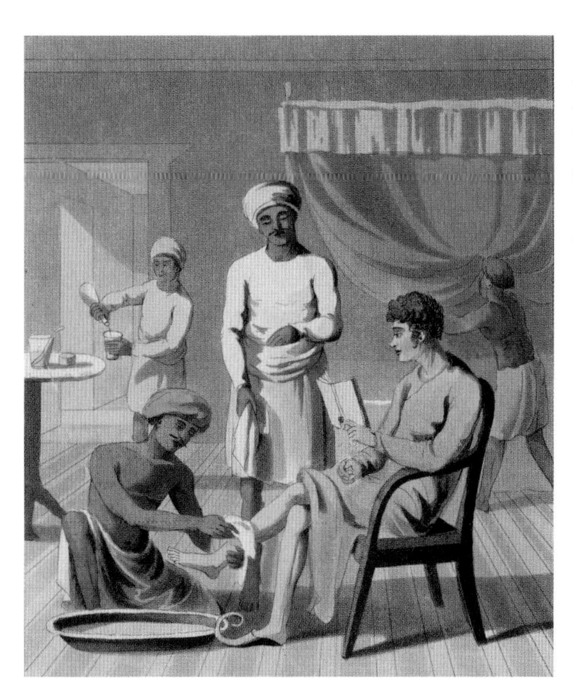

Sir Charles D'Oyly, *A Gentleman Dressing Attended by His Head Bearer and other Servants*, published in Thomas Williamson, *The Costume and Customs of Modern India* (1813).

In the eyes of the British landed elite, the wealthy nabobs returning to Britain brought with them greed, conspicuous consumption, and ambition learned and practised in India. Like Agnew's nabobs, these returnees threatened the status quo. Thomas Rumbold, for example, son of a purser, joined the East India Company as a teenager and was said to have accrued £1 million in the two years he served as governor of Madras. Nabobs used their savings to purchase country estates, build mansions and buy their way into Parliament. Unlike Agnew's nabobs, who were protesting against U.S. military activity in a faraway country of Southeast Asia, the British nabobs of the eighteenth and early nineteenth centuries were proponents of empire, of the right to extract wealth from the subcontinent. Back in Britain, the nabobs were called Anglo-Indians, which related not to racial descent but, rather, to having lived abroad.

While working and living in India, many of those associated with the East India Company adopted Indian customs, food and dress (in their homes, if not their offices), all usually denoted by the adjective

Unknown artist, *John Wombwell Smoking Hookah*, c. 1785–90, watercolour on paper.

'Mughal' and signifying the high fashion of the rulers' clothes and furnishings. Their robes and turbans, jewels and feathers, harems and gardens constituted an art of elite living. In a portrait from 1761, Josiah Reynolds's neighbour in London, Captain John Foote, poses in Mughal dress: robe, sash, shawl and feathered turban, as if he were in northern India. The muslin turban even has gold-embroidered flowers. In a conversation piece from 1790, John Mowbray, an East India Company civil servant in strict business dress and powdered wig, talks with his Indian trader, who is turbaned and his body swathed in layers of muslin.

While most Anglo-Indians returned with modest savings and displayed their cultural borrowing through pyjamas, cheroots, daily showers and building houses in the 'bungalow' (or Bengali) style, a few came home with enormous wealth. Most notorious among the latter were Robert Clive and Warren Hastings. Each held a high position in India, each returned to Britain immensely rich and each was subjected to parliamentary investigations as to whether they had committed malfeasance in India in order to accrue personal wealth. In an etching from 1768, James Gillray portrayed Hastings with a fortune acquired by corruption, maladministration and extortion in his work as governor general. The impeachment trial in the House of Lords continued for a decade, during which cartoonists had a field day. Gillray also made an etching of the British politician Henry Dundas, president of the Board of Control, which steadily increased government control over the East India Company. He wears a turban and kilt as he bestrides the gap between London and his company headquarters in Bengal. Dundas insisted that Britain oust the French from the south of India so that the British could monopolize trade. Lord Wellesley, the new governor general, successfully pursued this policy, and Dundas was awarded the rank of Viscount Melville. British anxiety over the domestic rise of nabobs involved a secondary fear: that Scottish nabobs were muscling in to the economic and political elite.

Prejudice against the nabobs was so strong that few returnees displayed their turbans and other Mughal clothes in public or even wore them at home. *The Nabob* (1788), a play by the popular playwright Samuel Foote, made those returning from India look ridiculous. There were aspects to mock, such as the mansion Sezincote in Gloucestershire, which had onion domes. These signs of new money spurred the eventual trial of Warren Hastings as well as legislation bringing the East India Company under closer parliamentary scrutiny.

As a youth, George Gordon Byron had a fancy for the Orient. He later claimed he had read 'all the books upon the east I could meet with, as well as Rycaut, before I was ten years old. I think the Arabian

James Gillray, *Dun-Shaw* (Henry Dundas), 1788, hand-coloured etching.

Nights first.' In 1802, in Bath with his mother, he entered the resort's party scene. To attend Lady Riddell's masquerade, he dressed up as a Turkish boy. He was coming into the house when someone tried to snatch the diamond crescent from his turban, but another guest intervened. Already, his peers were jealous.[10]

Byron played the part of his costume changes, imagining non-European modes of behaviour and values. At the age of twenty he received a bill from a Nottingham tailor requesting payment for a jacket and turban. On his first Grand Tour, in 1809, Byron called Albanian dress 'the most magnificent in the world'. He wrote to his mother about his purchase in a bazaar: 'I have some very "magnifique" Albanian dresses, the only expensive articles in this country[;] they cost 50 guineas each; have so much gold they would cost in England two hundred.' The costume he chose to wear to have his picture painted in 1814 was modelled on that of an Albanian noble warrior. He described it as 'as fine as a pheasant' and used it thirteen years later in a poem.[11]

Because of his affection for these stories, in his four *Turkish Tales* (1813–16) Byron imagined himself as an invincible hero in Middle Eastern conflicts. Scenarios featuring rebellious, fierce and liberated young men caught between cultures and nationalities, drinking 'life to the lees', propel these long poems. The turbans in *Turkish Tales* are not perfunctory. Both as costume and as symbols of male power and action, they come in such phrases as 'loftier turbans' and 'turbaned victors'. In *The Siege of Corinth*, the protagonist, Alp, is a renegade who has lost faith in his own European culture and fights for the 'turbaned horde', all the while dreaming of the tolerance of all creeds. The Christian maiden whose father had rejected Alp's suit tells him to 'dash that turban to earth, and sign/ The sign of the cross'. Alp, wearing a turban that 'on his hot brow pressed', goes into battle, focusing not on the large issue of allegiance but on loyalty to his fellow soldiers; he knew 'the best of his band' had fallen 'by the turbans that rolled on the sand'.

Selim in *The Bride of Abydos* falls in love with his half-sister Zuleika, a pasha's daughter living in the harem. She flees, Rapunzel-like, to make an escape with her lover, who is shot by her father. The dramatic last scene has them meet in a grotto, where Selim, disguised as a pirate ('His brow no high-crown'd turban bore'), reveals that Zuleika is not his half-sister after all. This gives them a moment of hope that the lovers can be together.

Don Juan is the longest and most popular of the *Turkish Tales*. Don Juan is depicted as sparkling like the Milky Way in a sartorial description that concludes: 'His turban, furl'd in many a graceful fold,/ An emerald aigrette with Haidee's hair in 't,/ Surmounted as its clasp – a glowing crescent,/ Whose rays shone ever trembling, but incessant.' Byron – who is appreciated for his satire as well as his sensuous language and air – returned in positive and negative ways to Eastern costume. In the story *Beppo*, Laura belongs to the elite who dress very well in a masque in the Venetian tradition. With a raised eyebrow Byron writes, 'She then surveys, condemns, but pities still/ Her dearest friends for being dress'd so ill./ One has false curls, another too much paint,/ A third – where did she buy that frightful turban?' Like other Romantics, Byron needed rapture. He lived in a stormy present of inner conflict and wild adventuring that he reconfigured in dramatic epic verse. No matter how far-fetched, a degree of verisimilitude comes from the poet's personal exploits, described in his letters, such as finding himself 'nearly lost in a Turkish ship of war', and wrapping himself 'in an Albanian capote and [lying] down on the deck waiting for the worst'.[12]

In the famous three-quarter portrait of Byron by Thomas Phillips, painted in 1813, the poet wears a turban, which suited the romantic image of his verse. It is elegant and flamboyant, and curves over his shoulder like a shawl, its reds and greens floating across his red and gold velvet jacket. Perhaps Byron wore it only once, since in May 1814 he sent part of the outfit to his friend Margaret Mercer Elphinstone, confidante of Queen Charlotte. He advised her to wear it to a costume

Thomas Phillips, *Lord Byron*, *c.* 1835, based on a work of 1813, oil on canvas.

party, and told her it would arrive when it had been properly laundered. Byron's clothes eventually went to Bowood House in Wiltshire, where they lay in a trunk until discovered in 1962; the estate put them in Bowood's exhibition hall, along with Napoleon's handkerchief and Queen Victoria's wedding chair.

By wearing a turban, Byron directed attention to his face. This supported his characterization as a poet, for he was known to be self-absorbed and theatrical in his passions. During his time as a student at the University of Cambridge, he was often absent. When another student was moving into Byron's rooms at Trinity College, a tutor cautioned him to be very careful with Byron's things. And because Byron took care with his Albanian clothes, they are preserved to this day.

In 1826–7 the 21-year-old Benjamin Disraeli, future prime minister of England, wrote *Vivian Grey*. The protagonist is a charmer and not a hero, but he speaks for all who travel across cultures when he ruminates, 'Like all great travellers I have seen more than I remember and remember more than I have seen.' Some travellers, instead of using the faculty of memory, become someone else in their travels, by 'going native'.

Like many unfortunate young men of his day, Joseph Pitts entered North Africa and the Muslim world under duress. In 1678 he and the rest of the crew of an English ship sailing to Spain were captured by Algerian pirates and sold into slavery. He was fourteen or fifteen years old. The son of one of his masters tried to force him to convert to Islam by beating him, to no avail. The son then dressed Pitts in Turkish clothes, presumably including a turban. But Pitts was steadfast in his born faith. He stated in his memoir, 'All the while I kept crying and told the patron that though he had changed my habit he could not change my heart.'[13] Fortunately, this owner sold Pitts to a kinder master, who took him on the hajj, which he described in accurate detail. In Mecca, the elderly gentleman manumitted Pitts, who promptly signed up for service on an Algerian naval ship docked in Jeddah. He eventually found his way to Smyrna in southern

Turkey, then back to England, where he wrote his *True and Faithful Account of the Religions and Manners of the Mohametans*, published in 1704.

Early in the nineteenth century, the Swiss explorer Jean Louis Burckhardt travelled to Arabia in full Turkish dress. An acquaintance aboard a ship sailing up the Nile described him as 'dressed in the commonest garments, as an Arab peasant or small trader, with a blue cotton blouse covering a coarse shirt, loose white trousers, and a common calico turban . . . he looked so completely like an Arab of the north . . . that few would have suspected him to be a Swiss.'[14] From Upper Egypt (the southern half of Egypt is so named because the Nile flows from south to north), Burckhardt sailed across the Red Sea and joined various caravans travelling to Medina and then Mecca. The traveller, who considered himself fully Muslim, visited the sacred grave of the Prophet in Medina and then performed the entire hajj in Mecca. He returned to Cairo, where he wrote his monumental *Travels in Arabia* (published posthumously in 1829) and lived indigenously until his early death at the age of 32.

Before Britain banned the slave trade in 1807, a number of British travellers purchased household slaves. These were European Christians captured by the Ottomans. Unlike the African slaves, shipped to the Americas, they did not endure forced labour in fields. But they were enslaved and often wore iron collars to discourage escape. In the 1820s one of the travellers, Charles Humphreys, described how he dressed in order to gain entrance to a slave market in Cairo:

> I am to become a Turk for my dress consisting in a large pair of trousers a yard and a half wide, a waistcoat with loose sleeves large enough to cover my hands and reach down to my instep, a large cloak, a pair of yellow slippers and a pair of red over them, a large sash round my waist and a turban made of seven yards of white muslin.[15]

John Beugo after Anthony van Dyck, *William Earl of Denbigh*, 1843, paper engraving.

The Orientalist and translator Edward William Lane, in three separate multi-year trips to Egypt, learned classical and spoken Arabic and wrote a bestseller, *An Account of the Manners and Customs of Modern Egyptians* (1836), *Arabic–English Lexicon* (1863–93; completed by his nephew) and a translation of *The Thousand and One Nights; or, The Arabian Nights' Entertainments* (1839–41). Both the *Manners and Customs* and the *Lexicon* have stayed in print. When Lane made his first trip to Egypt, he avoided the European quarter, where the merchants lived, and instead took up residence in a poor quarter, where he mastered the local Arabic dialect, adopted the lifestyle of the local people and dressed in a simple cotton outer garment (*gallabiyah*), vest and plain cotton turban. In the preface of *Manners and Customs,* he claimed, 'I have lived as they live, conforming with their general habits.' He emphasized his ability to ensure the trust of Muslims who were his informants, for example, by eating with his fingers, 'abstaining from wine and swine's flesh (both, indeed, loathsome to me)', and attending prayer services at the local mosque.[16] During the course of his daily excursions, Lane filled a sketchbook with drawings of scenes that provided illustrations for his books. In the last year of his first visit, he was sketching a slave market when a Greek girl caught his attention. He purchased her freedom and raised her in his Egyptian and English households. In 1840, when Nafeesah came of age at twenty, he married her.

On Lane's return to England after that first trip, his brother – a prominent artist – cast a life-size plaster sculpture of the scholar, which is now in the National Portrait Gallery, London. Although in Egypt Lane dressed as a common man, in the sculpture he wears the clothes of a Turkish gentleman of the contemporary ruling Mamluk class. The turban is silk, and the outer garment is heavier than the ordinary *gallabiyah.* In his left hand he holds a metal pen case, in his right a roll of paper, and a bound manuscript is placed towards the rear, doubtless his own *Description of Egypt,* which lingered on a publisher's desk for decades and achieved publication only posthumously.

On his second trip (1833–4) Lane took up residence, according to some reports, in a haunted house, which made it difficult to hire servants. One of his acquaintances was William Thompson, a Scottish soldier whom the ruling Mamluks had captured and enslaved in 1807. Thompson gained his freedom by converting to Islam and adopted the life of a Turkish grandee. *Manners and Customs* made Lane famous, but fame did not alter his scholarly life. In 1842 he returned to Egypt with Nafeesah as his wife, and with his sister and her two sons. Until 1849, when he returned to England, he gathered materials for his monumental *Arabic–English Lexicon,* and easily passed for an Egyptian. The *Lexicon* and his translation of the *Arabian Nights* occupied him fully for the rest of his life. Back home, his *gallabiyah*

Richard James Lane, *Edward William Lane*, 1829, plaster statue.

and turban remained in a trunk. Despite his renown as an author, he lived and dressed as an unassuming Victorian scholar.

Alexander Gardner, who became famous as the 'tartaned nabob', was the most remarkable adventurer in sartorial terms. If turbans were rare in Britain, they were common apparel among Anglo-Indians. Those who settled in India often cohabited with or even married Indian women, mostly Muslim, and raised families far from their places of birth. In the eighteenth century many Europeans, usually outside the political elites of their countries, migrated to India to better themselves. Some, such as Gardner, brought military skills, including how to manufacture arms and how to organize an effective army. By his own account, Gardner was born in 1801 on the western shore of Lake Superior in what is now Wisconsin. He died in the city of Jammu, India, in 1877. In between, again by his own account, he lived in Mexico, Philadelphia, England (but not Scotland), the Central Asian hinterland (now Kazakhstan and Turkestan) and finally in what is today India and Pakistan. Just where he travelled north on the Pamir Mountains is debated, and it is certain that he made up the Philadelphia residence on a whim. It is factual, however, that he left England as a late adolescent and never returned.

Gardner was the prototypical mercenary. His memoirs describe extensive travels in Central Asia in search of loot. Close brushes with death often left him wounded but a survivor – unlike a number of his adversaries. He entered the service of Maharaja Ranjit Singh in 1832, ending twelve years of 'romance and vicissitude'. By this time, Sikh men practised their religion by leaving their hair uncut, wearing a turban and carrying on their bodies a small dagger. During the Mughal Empire the Sikhs had established a reputation as skilled and brave warriors. During his service to Singh and other members of Singh's family, Gardner adopted their dress and religion fully, but avoided circumcision, which the Sikhs waived because of his age. Known as Gordana Sahib, Gardner found himself in the midst of the Great Game, the opposing strategies of the British and Russians to gain control of the Afghanistan route into South Asia. Although the terrain was rocky and harsh, Singh's army dressed in colourful uniforms of velvet and silk, and wore red, green and yellow turbans indicative of their military tasks.[17]

As an artillery expert, Gardner spent much of his time in the Sikh army taming unruly Pathans in the foothills of the Pamir Mountains. After the death of Ranjit Singh in 1839, the Sikh Kingdom declined into internecine struggles among Ranjit's many offspring. Gardner escaped court intrigues and worse by joining the Akali, an irregular core of fearless if poorly armed warriors loyal to Gulab Singh, who sided with the British in the final dissolution of the Sikh kingdom. The Akali fought with scimitars and bow and arrows. On their tall turbans they fastened their bows and sharp quoits, which they hurled at the enemy. After a climactic battle, the Akali carried about the Sikh

Kingdom the decapitated heads of Ranjit's loyalists until Gardner 'managed with great difficulty to secure the heads and to send them to Gulab Singh'.[18]

With the Sikh Kingdom in disarray, Gardner found a position as officer in the British army. In the 1860s he settled in Srinagar, then as now a popular retirement territory with its rivers, lakes and high, verdant valleys. There he encountered the 79th Cameron Highlanders, whom the British government had sent to shore up security in the Punjab after the Indian Rebellion of 1857. Gardner was semi-retired, living with his (at least) seventh wife, a Punjabi, in partial reclusion. The wife, whose name Gardner does not mention in his memoirs, lived in total purdah, never appearing in public or at home in the presence of guests. To support the Highlanders in their colourful uniforms, Srinagar tailors imported bolts of their distinctive tartan. Although he never set foot on Scottish soil, Gardner embraced the tartan from turban to trousers.

In the late 1860s and '70s Gardner was a celebrity among fellow world travellers and adventurers, some of whom made a special trip to visit him in Kashmir. One such person was Charles Longfellow, son of the much-loved American poet Henry Wadsworth Longfellow. To prepare himself for meeting the Muslim convert, Charles read and brought on his travels the Qur'an and a biography of the Prophet Muhammad. He and Gardner attended a Hindu festival, at which Gardner climbed onto the stage to dance with the women performers. Charles recorded that his host wore 'a red coat with green epaulettes and gold turban'.[19] Born a Catholic, Gardner wore his religion lightly but colourfully.

Other nabobs entered India's markets as traders, part of the chain of supply for cottons and silks and for such spices as pepper, cloves, ginger and cinnamon, and for gems mined from India's earth. These adventurers did not work for the East India Company or for the likes of Henry Dundas. They tended to be self-made men from middle-class Irish and Scots backgrounds who worked for India's local

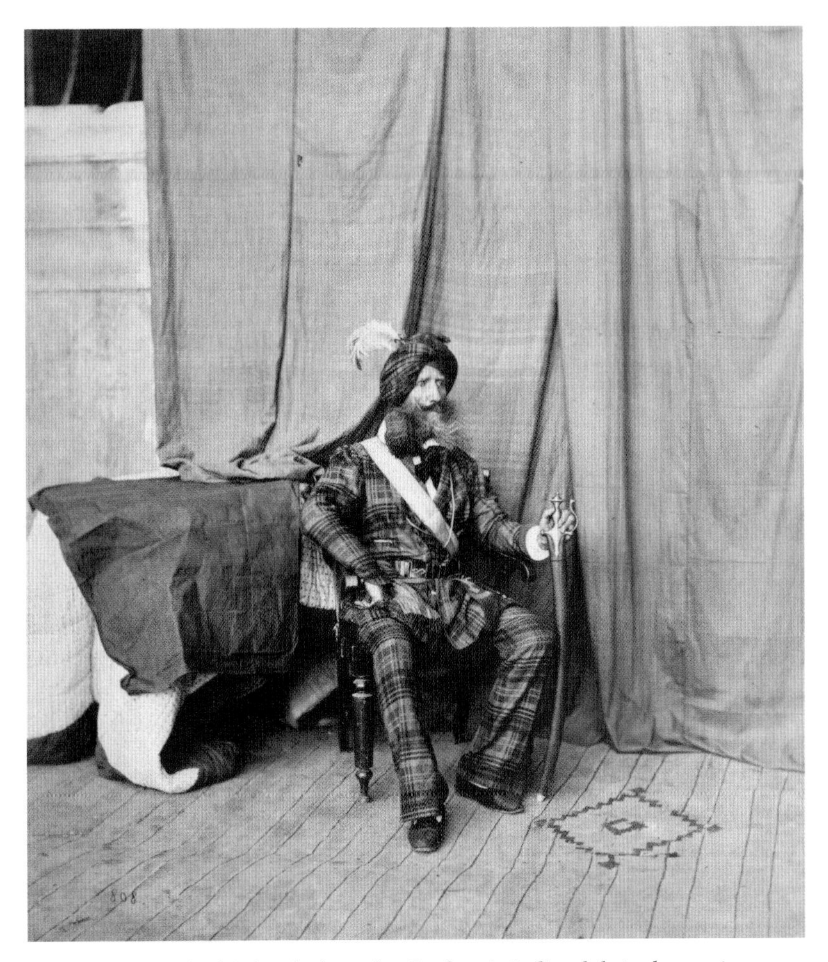

Photograph of Colonel Alexander Gardner in India while in the service of Maharaja Gulab Singh, 1850, albumen print.

rulers, and one may assume that many adopted culture, local customs and languages, the last sometimes fluently.

A gifted linguist, Richard Burton mastered spoken as well as classical Arabic. Unlike Lane, he thrived as an explorer. While in the East India army, he worked as a spy in the Sindh to investigate whether the British should reform such domestic practices as the right of a husband to hang an unfaithful wife, such sexual practices as brothels of young boys and such penal practices as a man condemned to death purchasing a substitute.[20] He did this undercover work disguised as an Afghan merchant, his head dressed in a colourful, many-layered turban of the kind favoured by his new profession. This was his disguise on his first big expedition, which took him to Arabia and the holy cities in the 1850s. Like Burckhardt, Burton passed as a pilgrim and recorded the events in detail. Outside Mecca, he wore a green turban, a mark of descendants of the Prophet Muhammad. Since the green turban invited genealogical enquiries, Burton was under much closer scrutiny than Burckhardt. His book, *A Personal Narrative of a Pilgrimage to El-Medinah and Meccah* (1855) – written quickly in the first edition and edited more carefully by his wife, Isabel, in later editions – was notable for Burton's running commentary on places and people, and his second disguise as a physician, which gained him entry into the harems of Medina and Mecca. His descriptions of the harems were so graphic that his publisher insisted that he relegate them to footnotes in Latin.

As soon as his *Pilgrimage* was published, Burton organized an expedition to Abyssinia, again in the disguise of an Afghan merchant, including 'a turban of portentous circumference' rather than the smaller Arab turbans.[21] When he was 41, Burton married Isabel Arundell, who had admired and even longed for him for a decade. As a result of his famous search for the source of the Nile, both his health and his bank account were broken. Isabel was well enough placed socially and tireless in her promotion of her husband that she secured him diplomatic positions in East Africa and Brazil, both unsuitable for a wife. Her third attempt allowed her to join Burton in Damascus, and these were their happiest years, during which they both 'went native'. In public, a turban enhanced Burton's craggy looks while Isabel, dressed in baggy trousers and a burnous (cloak), passed as his son.[22] In her biography of her husband, Isabel described a rooftop meal with Abd el-Kadir, the exiled former leader of much of central North Africa, Richard in 'snowy white, both turban and burnous'.[23] Isabel was also an adept horsewoman who could ride with the Burtons' English compatriots and Arab hosts. The couple returned to England for good in 1874. He wrote a *Kama Sutra* and *The Perfumed Garden of Shaykh Nefzawi*, both erotica, translated the *Arabian Nights* and founded the Kama Shastra Society to publish and privately circulate among its members classic texts forbidden by the Obscene Publications Act of 1857. Isabel unfortunately destroyed much of her husband's collection of and notes on erotica in an attempt to protect his reputation. The couple now lie in coffins in a stone tomb shaped like a Bedouin tent, in the churchyard of St Mary Magdalen, Mortlake, southwest London.

In his book *Orientalism* (1978), the academic Edward Said accused scholars of the Middle East of perpetrating colonialist falsehoods: for example, that contemporary Islam was essentially frozen in a medieval scholasticism that the West had abandoned; that numerous paintings of Turkish daily life portrayed Turks as idle and lascivious; and that Burton and other scholars were really British agents. Said criticized Lane's living as a local while residing in Egypt as a 'disguise'. In Said's view, these Westerners were using their Orientalist skills to demean their objects of study, art and travel. The adventurers and nabobs of this chapter certainly did enjoy the privilege of empire. Burton worked for the British government; Gardner was a mercenary. Their appropriations of Middle Eastern languages and clothes served imperial interests. Today, many scholars and policymakers would view their work as inappropriate for the twenty-first century. But Lane was a dedicated scholar with no direct involvement with the imperial bureaucracy, and yes, he married a girl he rescued and raised to marriageable age.

Jean-Étienne Liotard, *Fourth Earl of Sandwich*, n.d., oil on canvas.

4

Masques and Turquerie

In the eighteenth century some Baroque artists pushed the symbolism and visuality of the turban. In *The Presentation in the Temple* (1738), Christian Wilhelm Ernst Dietrich, son of a Weimar court painter, showed the Holy Family dwarfed by a Jewish potentate wearing a turban hitched up on a tower of fabric. His assistant wears a full turban knotted at the top, while another man's wraps around a cap.

As more French people travelled to the Ottoman Empire, Turkish-themed masquerades abandoned allegory for a more accurate replication of Turkish costumes and manners. Especially influential was the publication in 1714 of the *Recueil de cent estampes . . .* (Collection of 100 Prints), which contained detailed costume plates from many parts of the empire executed by the French-Flemish artist Jean Baptiste Vanmour, a significant precursor of Orientalism and Turquerie. Born into a carpenter's family in the lacemaking centre of Valenciennes in northern France, he had the good fortune to apprentice in the workshop of an outstanding artist, Jacques-Albert Gérin. Among Gérin's works is *The Magus Balthazar* (*c.* 1700), depicting an eminently wealthy and intense African man wearing a voluminous bejewelled silver turban.

Some travellers to the East journeyed explicitly on assignment to bring back views. Vanmour spent 38 years painting various peoples in the extensive Ottoman Empire. By the time he travelled, the wars between the Ottomans and Europeans had concluded and trade connections dominated. He depicted a variety of turbans among the many kinds of headgear worn by Jews, Armenians and Hungarians as well as Muslims of different vocations from across the empire. In one painting, *Dinner at the Palace in Honour of an Ambassador* (1700), the sultan wears a headdress 0.6 metre (2 ft) high that looks like ladyfingers arranged in a circle. Vanmour would not have drawn in the harem, but there is an exactitude about his work that evinces the accuracy of the costumes. He drew an unveiled Greek woman inside her home, her hair piled in a snood. Even though he portrayed her in her own home, the image may have spread a false idea that women of the harem wore turbans, thus exerting an influence on later European fashions.

Recueil de cent estampes was commissioned by Charles, comte de Ferriol, the French ambassador to Constantinople from 1699 to 1711. The count was interested in the culture of the East, and Vanmour, who had graduated from the French academy in Rome, gave him the illustrations he sought. The collection of engravings with explanatory text familiarized Europeans with life at the palace and in the bazaar with such events as weddings and funerals, and with the distinctions among the clothes of the various ethnic groups. The turbans shown in the book are worn by commoners and men of high status, from the simple turban of a *barbier ambulatoire* (itinerant hairdresser) to the white turban over a red cap with gold sequins of the grand vizier's valet. The book was quickly translated from the French into German and English, and its copperplate engravings were sold and circulated separately. Whereas before the *Cents estampes* high-level masqueraders were dependent on private experts to assist them, after its publication literate Europeans had easy access to accurate images of clothes of the extended Ottoman Empire. It was so influential that elements of Turkish style were integrated into European music, dance and theatre. In recognition of Vanmour's achievement, he was granted the title of Peintre Ordinaire du Roi en Levant (Painter to the King in the East) by Louis XV in 1725.

The Genevan artist Jean-Étienne Liotard worked in Constantinople and then in Jassy (Iași, Romania) and Moldavia between 1738 and 1743. In the late 1830s, disappointed with his career in Paris, he had gone with the French ambassador to the Neapolitan court. There he had met William Ponsonby (the future 2nd Earl of Bessborough) and John Montagu (the 4th Earl of Sandwich), two English tourists who employed him to travel with them to the Ottoman Empire in 1738. Liotard arrived in Constantinople the year after Vanmour. Montagu, who didn't want to stay with the others, persuaded Liotard to accompany him to the Levant.

The sources for Liotard's drawings were the coloured engravings by Vanmour, Persian miniatures and pictures he found in the bazaar. He painted both elite Ottomans and Europeans, and dressed like a Turk for the rest of his life. He went to courts all over Europe in his Ottoman attire and wearing a beard when most men were clean-shaven. He insisted in his portraits that his sitters could be both Europeans and Turks. Inspired by Persian representational art, he painted in a style that was subtly two-dimensional and smooth-surfaced, with brilliant colours.

In the second half of the seventeenth century the English philosopher John Locke challenged the medieval union of Church and State. He argued that religion was mostly personal and thrived in a non-official realm of believers. In his *Letter Concerning Toleration* (1689), he laid the foundation for a fundamental separation of Church and State in England, including those from 'turbaned nations'. Resident Muslims were few in England, but a visit from a Moroccan ambassador in 1682 revealed to the English that Christians worshipped freely in the ambassador's country. Although far from asserting the oneness of the different religions, Locke called for similar religious freedom for Jews, Muslims and Dissenters in England, as long as they were law-abiding.[1] In a letter, he noted that Muslims customarily wore their turbans to prayer services in the mosque, whereas most Christians removed their hats when worshipping. Locke's letter stirred up considerable opposition among the English clergy, and in response he relegated to the background the sharp contrasts between Islamic and Christian theologies, bringing to the foreground the sincerity of Muslims and Christians in their worship and daily life. This despite persistent fears that the Ottoman Turks would continue to expand into Central Europe, fears that subsided after 1683, when the Turks gave up their siege of Vienna.

In the eighteenth century the phrase 'exchanging the hat for the turban' was a common description of conversion to Islam: the hat representing Christianity, the turban Islam. Claude Alexandre, comte de Bonneval, prominently gave up his hat for a turban. He was a French aristocrat and soldier of fortune, and the first European to exert military influence in the Ottoman Empire. Descending from an old family in Limousin, Bonneval counted Louis XIV's nephew Philippe d'Orléans as his boyhood playmate. Yet when he served as an officer in the king's royal guard, he disobeyed the minister of war and was compelled to flee the country. He fought under the Austrian flag as a major general with Prince Emmanuel of Savoy, then saw his chance with the Ottomans. In Constantinople in 1730 he converted to Islam, shaved his head and donned a turban. He grew a beard to complement the turban and changed his name to Ahmed Pasha. In public he wore silk tunics, long fur-trimmed coats and curly-toed shoes. He was a two-tailed pasha, meaning he could display two horsetails on his turban and military standard. His life continued to be a dangerous game, yet he managed to navigate Persian and Ottoman politics and parlay with France and the Habsburg powers for the rest of his life.[2]

Bonneval's identity moved between East and West. Of this the turban was a key symbol, as it would be from the eighteenth century all the way to T. E. Lawrence, for travellers who had a psychological or practical desire to move from culture to culture. Voltaire called Bonneval the 'Comte-pacha de Bonneval'. His Ottoman persona was as functional as his European-ness. Bonneval told Giacomo Casanova, 'I had to say that God is God and Mahomet was His Prophet. Who

Andrew Miller after Johann Heinrich Schröder, *Count Bonaval*, 1744, mezzotint on paper.

knows whether I thought so. I wear the turban as I would wear a uniform.'[3] As Ahmed Pasha, the count also assured his brother, 'I am the same Comte de Bonneval as before. Clothes don't make the monk.'[4]

An early portrait shows Bonneval in a generic turban from the *Recueil de cent estampes*. In about 1740 he sat for Liotard, who depicted him with a more colourful, squat turban, 'a thick cloth, twisted repeatedly around a central striped head-covering.'[5] Voltaire provided piquant remarks about this controversial person. After Bonneval had been temporarily exiled during political upheavals in Constantinople, Voltaire commented, 'I am only surprised that, having been exiled to Asia Minor, he didn't then go serve the Sophy of Persia, Thamas Kouli-Khan; he could have had the pleasure of continuing straight on to China, quarrelling successively with all the ministers of state along the way. His head appears to me to have had more need of brains than of a turban.'[6]

Like many travellers to the East, this chimerical adventurer provoked wide interest in Europe. Factitious memoirs and gossip had it that he was circumcised – a common requirement for converts – in middle age. The count vacillated between denial and silence. Then, in 1744, knowing this would spread the news, he wrote to Voltaire that he had received a waiver of circumcision out of respect for his age (55) when he converted.

By the mid-eighteenth century the balance of power in Europe operated with France and her allies on one side, and England and her allies on the other, sometimes in formal alliances and sometimes not. While the Ottoman Empire did not have a formal alliance with France, the Turks traded with that country and shared its wariness of Austria and Russia. A system of French spies called the *secret du Roi* (king's secret) had been set up in 1745 to keep an eye on the complicated politics of the region, fictionalized memorably by Ivo Andrić in *The Bosnian Chronicle* (1945). In the novel the French and Austrian consuls pass each other in their carriages or on horseback on the road, unsure whether to acknowledge each other. The diplomats are in the dark about their roles because they haven't received the latest instructions from their countries. Writes Andrić, 'There was plainly no such thing as a road leading onward; in reality all roads led one around in a circle, like those tricky mazes in Eastern tales.'[7]

Their predicament might have been that of Charles Gravier, comte de Vergennes. When the French ambassador who had been serving at the Porte, the comte des Alleurs, died in December 1754, the French needed to designate an envoy quickly. Vergennes was young but trained in diplomacy by an uncle who was an intimate of highly placed officials in Versailles. Thus, Vergennes was named Louis XV's minister plenipotentiary (a step below ambassador) to the Porte. He had two weeks to settle his affairs in France, be fitted for a wardrobe and choose presents for the sultan and the Turkish ministers and other officials. However, his gift allowance was inadequate, and he asked for a delay. Then the reigning sultan, Mahmud I, suddenly died.

After he had been appointed ambassador in 1747, the comte des Alleurs spent six whole months and a fortune to outfit himself to impress the sultan. A royal entrance, he felt, was the key to success. He lived lavishly in Constantinople and left his wife with major debts on his passing. After Vergennes arrived, he assisted his predecessor's widow. By 1760 he was well established in the Ottoman capital and sat for a portrait by one of the European artists who plied their trade in the Ottoman territories. In the seated portrait, he is clean-shaven as a European, but his magnificent outfit bespeaks a love of Turkey. There is a green enamelled, jewelled dagger in his pocket and in his left hand he holds prayer beads. He is gorgeously arrayed in richly layered garments. Beneath a marigold-yellow silk tunic decorated with red roses, he wears a pale blue underdress (*jama*) with a similar fabric of pink bouquets. His rose wool coat has a thick border of white fur and more surrounding him than worn is a mantle of dark fur. While the count appears self-assured and lordly, a strain is perceptible in his neck. On his head perches not an everyday turban but one half a metre (2 ft) tall that he must keep straight by his posture, helped by gold straps at both sides. The large white foundation turban rests on a quilted red cap, and a second pillbox 'base turban' surmounts the white one.

The details of ambassadorial dress had as much importance in Constantinople as at Versailles. When told that a fur-lined rose-coloured robe was a privilege of high Turkish officials and important ambassadors and therefore unacceptable for the newly arrived count to wear at an audience with Sultan Osman III, Vergennes said he would ask Louis XV how to proceed, and that swept the problem away. Over coffee, Vergennes conversed with the sultan through a lattice on a kiosk. This was unusual, writes the historian Orville T. Murphy:

> With the formalities over, servants entered and Vergennes rose to permit the precious fur-lined robe to be placed on his shoulders. Then he once again took his place on the taboret. Coffee, sherbet, and perfumed water were again offered. In due course Vergennes took his leave, but not before noting that the ceremonial turbans worn by the *Grand Vazir* and the Chief Usher were an honour ordinarily accorded only to ambassadors.[8]

When he was recalled to France in 1768, the count returned to his estate in Burgundy, happy to forget the court. In 1774 he became foreign minister and had a role in French support for American independence from the British Crown.

Turquerie flared as one of the great interior decorative styles important to the upper classes in the early eighteenth century. Attention was given to that most practical item of furniture in a draughty home: the bed. An eccentric example of Turquerie is Prince Eugene of Savoy's *Türkenbett* in the Augustinian abbey of St Florian, Upper Austria. Austria had a long tradition of sculptors working with wood, which was often gilded and, in Baroque style, painted. The prince's bed depicted a multinational war and celebrated European victories against the Ottomans. Two painted bedposts represent Ottoman warriors, fearsome compared with the conventions of the fundamentally Rococo style of Turquerie. The left-hand one, an officer, wears a red jacket with golden borders and a turquoise turban decorated with a golden feather. The right-hand one wears simpler clothes, and his hands are behind his back. Far from light-hearted, the Turks' facial expressions are like a remembered nightmare, while at the same time each carving is a beautifully painted sculpture. Their postures indicate that they have been vanquished while fighting. At the head of the bed stand two Roman soldiers with cuirasses and lances. They seem to act as guards for the person sleeping in the bed.

The traditional connection of the bed with Prince Eugene of Savoy is in line with the militarism of its decoration. Prince Eugene, brought up at the court of Louis XIV, became a lauded general of the Holy Roman Empire. For his part in repelling the Ottomans at Vienna he received a large area in Lower Austria (the northeast corner of the country), which he enlarged by buying more areas, and which became his country residence. In Vienna Prince Eugene owned the Winter Palace, nowadays part of the Ministry of Finance, and, later on, the Belvedere as a Summer or Garden Palace, both built on his behalf. Tradition has it that the Austrian commoners took up a collection and gifted the bed to Eugene. However, despite its name, the bed was never in the general's possession. Rather, the St Florian Monastery commissioned it in about 1710 for furnishing the imperial rooms, built to accommodate the emperor and empress if they visited on their travels.[9]

In 1721 Sultan Ahmet III sent an ambassador, Mehmet Çelebi Efendi, to the court of Louis XV. The king, but a boy of eleven, was pleased with the ambassador, who stayed eleven months in Paris – the longest stay of any ambassador from the East. The king's painter, Antoine Coypel, painted the ceremony of the young king receiving the ambassador. Louis sits on a platform above the floor from where the visitors look on. One of the embassy officials doffs his turban and bows; the ambassador keeps his on. Çelebi and his entourage were featured in Parisian newspapers, and the Ottoman visit became the subject of art and tapestries. His father was a Janissary, the head keeper of the sultan's mastiffs, and Çelebi's permanent position was in the Janissary corps. Learned and wise, he was the sultan's chief accountant at the time of his assignment as Ottoman ambassador to France. Aristocrats of Versailles rented windows in Paris to watch the handsome ambassador ride into the city in his stylish carriage. He was depicted wearing heavy silk and fur robes, Turkish slippers and a white turban larger than that of the others in the *ambassade*. In a painting by Pierre Gobert commissioned by the king in 1724, Çelebi's outstanding feature is a wide, high forehead, which favours the massive white turban he wears over his cap. A ribbon, possibly velvet, is tied around the turban's girth. Çelebi admired the stage sets and jewelled costumes at Paris's theatres, and remarked how the actors each played a single part. The main results of his visit were twofold. On the Turkish side this was the earliest sustained encounter with French culture *sur place*.

Turkish bed in the Prince Eugene Room in the St Florian Monastery, *c.* 1710; photograph 1999.

Çelebi brought back information about printing, and subsequently an Ottoman printing press was established. On the French side the fashion for Turquerie engaged the French elite.

The year of the historic *ambassade* was also the year of the birth of Jeanne-Antoinette Poisson, who became Louis XV's long-term fashion-setting mistress. The association of the king and his mistress began with Orientalizing, which must have made it a soft spot in their hearts. At a masked ball celebrating the marriage of the Dauphin, Louis, to the Spanish Infanta, Maria Teresa Rafaela, the king and seven of his friends dressed comically as papier-mâché yew trees, clipped so that they resembled turbaned heads. Some masqueraders sported genuine-looking Turkish clothing, while other guests wore exotic melange costumes. No one else seemed as well disguised as the yew trees with their oversized turbaned heads, although the costume proved uncomfortably warm for dancing and the king took off the yew-tree head as the ball progressed.

The ball came to be known as *le bal des ifs*, the ball of the yew bushes. A court artist, Charles-Nicolas Cochin, gave a very different look to the turbans in two different engravings. In one, the prepossessing faux Turks have enormous turbans shaped like wrapped flowerpots on their heads. In the other the turbans are also prominent, but they transform the courtiers into topiary, matching the sculpted shrubs of the parterre below the Hall of Mirrors at Versailles.

Jeanne-Antoinette moved up in name and rank, and was soon ennobled as the royal mistress, the marquise de Pompadour. Her position granted her a residence between Paris and Versailles that she named Bellevue and furnished on a harem theme. Her bedroom, known as the *chambre du Roi*, looked out over the terrace, with a view of the Seine. On the mantlepiece sat two large Sèvres vases, lilac with medallions depicting seven scenes. The fireplace's andirons, now at the Louvre, were in a Rococo form of stylized male and female Turks. A painting by Charles-André Vanloo, *Sultan's Wife Drinking Coffee* (1755), discreetly references Madame de Pompadour. In her boudoir, Louis XV's mistress sits with her black seamstress, fabric on arm and lap, who pours her a dainty cup of coffee. The sultana/ Pompadour wears high on her head a turban graced with a rose, and the seamstress wears a simple turban hanging over her ear to her breast.

These decorative paintings were suggestive of the *vie intérieure* or fabled *birun* of Topkapı Palace in Constantinople. Before working on the triptych for Bellevue, Vanloo had already made Turkish subject paintings for the king at Versailles. He presented Madame de Pompadour as a sultana with pearls woven into her braids, strands of jewels on her headpiece and a rose tucked into its knot, a subversion of the severe etiquette that reigned at Versailles. Vanloo apparently used Vanmour's engravings as an important source; however, he also consulted a rare manuscript of Turkish paintings of the court in Constantinople that Çelebi had presented to the king in 1721. Perrin Stein, Curator of Drawings and Prints at the Metropolitan Museum of Art in New York, makes an important point that holds true for the European fashion for Turquerie in decor and clothes: 'Madame de Pompadour was not concerned with verisimilitude as we would define it today, but rather with a rich evocation of Turkey created with available luxury goods, both imported and of French manufacture.'[10]

The marquise retained her influence with her royal lover after their sexual relationship ended. Her Turkish boudoir exhibited that hold. She died in 1764, but boudoirs decorated with Turkish motifs gained popularity during the rest of the Bourbon period. According to Stein, 'Madame de Pompadour's Turkish bedroom at Bellevue is of unique importance for both its early date and . . . its incorporation of a personalized programmatic content.'[11] The Gobelins tapestry manufactory produced colourful cartoons from Vanloo's designs, and the royal factories of Denmark and Germany borrowed the motif of a sultana and a Moor from him as well. The Moor was always colourful, his turban as likely to be red and yellow as white.

In European eyes, he was understood to be a free person, so that the iconography of the porcelain or textile art objects did not reduce the sultana's consort to a slave. In the Gobelin tapestries, the men from exotic lands were sometimes wise, sometimes despotic, farcical or libertine with several wives, while the turban remained a visual separating device.

Among European travellers, the architect Barthélemy-Michel Hazon assumed a pronounced swagger in his Turkish attire. Portrayed by Joseph-Marie Vien in the mid-eighteenth century, Hazon emerges from the mist of an imaginary city. A superintendent of the palace

Charles-André Vanloo, *Sultan's Wife Drinking Coffee*, 1755, oil on canvas.

Joseph-Marie Vien, *Barthélemy-Michel Hazon in the Costume of a Turkish Mufti*, 1748, oil on canvas.

under Louis XV and Louis XVI, he was a small man, but he wears an imposing white turban as if he were a mufti. Taller than a top hat, the ornate turban is also heavier than a real person could sustain, especially on horseback. Hazon sports a long, curly white beard, wears a white turban, a fur-trimmed overtunic and a white caftan, and carries an elephant folio book. Under the patronage of Madame de Pompadour, Hazon was studying architecture at the Academy of France in Rome in 1748 when he switched the anticipated Roman theme for a costume party to a more ambitious and extravagant Turkish event which took place in February as part of the students' carnival. Masques were a great courtly and public diversion, and celebrations before the Lenten season were famous for their elaborately staged and costumed pageants.

Masques harked back to Voltaire's play on freedom of speech, *Le Fanatisme, ou Mahomet le Prophète,* first performed in 1741. Horse-drawn floats carried the students gaudily bedizened to evoke sultans and sultanas, viziers, eunuchs and other stock figures borrowed from the Ottoman court. There were even *soi-disant* Turkish courtiers parading with the sultan on a pilgrimage to Mecca. Pope Benedict XIV was said to have participated incognito. Vien made engravings of designs for Voltaire's tragedy in a series called *La Caravane du Sultan à la Mecque* before he did the 32 costume designs. The turbans worn by such characters as the Mughal ambassador and his wife were attention-grabbing interpretations with feathers galore. The French ambassador to Rome praised the spectacle and invited the masqueraders to be his guests for a banquet followed by a ball.

Turkish *galanteries* appeared on Sèvres vases when Madame du Barry became the last official mistress of Bourbon France. Her tea table, dated 1774, has six porcelain plaques with cartouches and a central scene of a *musicale* in which the female figures are in French fashions while the men sport turbans. A gilded pair of consoles from 1780, also owned by her, are supported by two black men in gold turbans, their bodies muscular and naked to the hips. Yet below the hips, the men have fish tails suitable for the sea but not the earth.

Just as Queen Anne of Great Britain and Ireland had her own and her ladies' skin darkened for a court masquerade, in Madame du Barry's time having a slave with very black skin was prized. At the court of Versailles, the royal mistress accentuated her blondeness by owning a dark-skinned slave, who went everywhere with her. As a young boy, Louis-Benoit Zamor was sold into slavery in Chattogram, Bengal, a depot for the slave trade when the British East India Company had de facto political control of eastern India. He was a gift to the royal favourite, Louis XIV's godson, the third Duc de Richelieu. Madame du Barry was under the illusion that Zamor was from Africa, that region being more mysterious to French aristocrats than India. She had him baptized Louis-Benoit in 1770, when he was about ten, in the church of Notre-Dame de Versailles. She played the role of godmother, and he was dressed in a silvery white coat with silver buttons, belt and sabre. In a portrait of him that may include that very costume, Zamor is luxuriously arrayed, with a disdainful gaze. Madame du Barry wrote in her memoirs how attached she was to Zamor, that she loved him second-best after her pet dog Dorinne: 'The second object of my regard was Zamor, a young African lad, full of intelligence and mischief: simple and independent by nature, however, wild as his country. Zamor believed himself to be the equal of everyone he met, barely deigning to recognize the king himself as his superior.'[12] At Madame du Barry's royal suppers Zamor carried trays of refreshments. He also held up his lady's parasols and dress trains, and rolled himself on the carpets, both attendant and jester, an embodiment of the Rococo and its exquisite porcelains with both delicious and absurd subject-matter. A painting of the enslaved boy and the countess is in her bedroom at the Château de Louveciennes. In it Zamor, who has brought the countess a demitasse of coffee, gazes at her with apparent devotion.

As an Oriental plaything Zamor was subjected to teasing by the guests. The countess clearly liked to dress him up, and an anonymous portrait of him some years older shows him in turban and full

Anonymous, *Zamor*, *c.* 1770, oil painting.

regalia. The turban matches the jacket under his frock coat; it is red with a white jewelled sash at the base. Its design and the white, red and black feather perched on it, garlanded with pearls, look invented by a milliner. His gorgeousness parodied the excesses of the court.

The way the fortunes of countess and slave sorted out in the French Revolution involved a dramatic reversal. Apparently self-educated, Zamor read many books, especially philosophy. He was impressed with the ideas of Jean-Jacques Rousseau. He knew slavery was an absolute evil and that he deserved the personal autonomy that Rousseau said was the right of human beings. When the Revolution started, Zamor became the secretary of the Comité de Surveillance Revolutionnaire for the district of Madame du Barry's chateau. She escaped to England, but returned in order to recover her jewels after a theft. Zamor warned her how unwise this was but, obsessed with her diamonds, she ignored him. In September 1793 he informed on her. The countess was arrested but released, and, in a fury at Zamor, gave him three days to leave her house. Zamor brought more charges against her, as a result of which she was arrested a second time, in December. She was subsequently tried and executed. In the trial papers Zamor's birthplace became known as he signed '*Louis-Benoit, né au Bengale dans l'inde*'.

When the Girondins gained a brief ascendancy in the National Assembly, Zamor was suspected of being Madame du Barry's accomplice. He spent six weeks in jail and afterwards fled France, not returning until 1815, after the fall of Napoleon's First Empire. He bought a house near the Latin Quarter in Paris and became a schoolteacher, by all accounts a strict one. After his death in 1820, in the popular imagination his name conjured up not as one might anticipate liberation from slavery, but rather maliciousness, a tale of a devious traitor's betrayal of a frivolous but kindly countess.

Influenced by the comedies with Oriental themes popular in the second half of the eighteenth century, the comte d'Artois (Louis XVI's brother) employed the brothers Jules-Hugues and Jean-Siméon

Rousseau to embellish the doors of Versailles palace with Neoclassical arabesques of flowers and pearls, turbaned figures, mermaids and garlands. On the upper half of a door a sultan or pasha sits on a throne surmounted by a crescent moon, with two odalisques offering him a long-stemmed pipe. Over the medallion a blue-eyed figure standing on a garland plays a stringed instrument and kicks up his heels. He looks pleased with himself. His turban is a red pillbox with a white sash around it. The turbaned figures on the painted panels bespeak jocularity. The fat-cheeked little pashas are as impish and benevolent-looking as Santa Clauses. The pashas were reminiscent of other Orientalist scenes of sensual pleasure and gallivanting, including the frivolities on Sèvres china and in such paintings as *La Boisson Froide* (The Cold Drink, 1750) by court painter Christophe Huet.

It is known that Marie Antionette was pregnant with her first child at the time, so perhaps he designed the Fontainebleau wall paintings on his own. The cabinet had a door panel painted with a dark-skinned turbaned figure with one red and one blue-green drooping feather, surrounded by dainty, ornate arabesques. Carrying the motif of the turban further, the columns of the marble fireplace were adorned with spirals of gilt-bronze with turbans at the top. The handles of the shovel and tongs were modelled as blackamoor heads. D'Artois's own taste in apparel embodied the Rococo fantasy of civilized frivolity; his state clothes when he was crowned King Charles x in 1814 continued the excesses of the old court.

In July 1788 three ambassadors from the Sultan of Mysore arrived in Paris to ask Louis xvi for an alliance against Britain. They stayed until October. They were the last ambassadors to come from the East to Versailles, this being but one year before the storming of the Bastille. A gouache by Charles-Eloi Asselin depicts them promenading in the rose garden at Saint-Cloud, west of Paris, among the fashionable Parisians and Middle Eastern textile-sellers. Parisians were fascinated and the three were seen all over the city (the *Journal de Paris* reported on them daily) and the visit generated a mania for all things Indian.

Soon after the ambassadors reached Paris, a printing firm brought out an engraving of the diplomatic exchange. The ambassadors are shown full-length, with feathered turbans and clothes adorned by jewels and buttons, all much fancier than those usually worn by Eastern officials of their type. What they wore was closer to the attire represented in Vanmour's illustrations of more than fifty years earlier. Although Vanmour himself had carefully distinguished between different professional and ethnic groups in his compendium, artists who later used his plates as source material often elided these distinctions to create more generally exotic figures, as was the case with the Mysore delegation.

During Louis XV's reign, turbaned figures on decorations had become less realistic and more romanticized, with artists and craftspeople improvising on the proverbial Turks seen in albums and engravings. The same design sources that were used for wall paintings and *papier peint* (patterned wallpaper) in France appeared on Meissen and Delft figures actively enjoying themselves. These were cunning and absurd confections that caught the imagination of all Europe as the production of porcelain spread. At the venerated and trendsetting Meissen factory in Germany, Johann Joachim Kändler – the court sculptor of Augustus II 'the Strong' – created models that were used to make porcelain for the royal court. These were fantasy confections with themes of the Oriental life. Kändler worked from engraved sources, which he modified for decorative value. For example, his images of children dressed up in parodies of Ottoman costume showed them as dwarfed by their turbans.

German factories produced porcelains of Turkish subjects, often taking the form of frolicsome grotesques. For example, a porcelain figural group of 1767 includes a moustachioed sultan in a carnival of colours, including a turban striped with metallic paint and sporting a great bush of red and aqua plumes. A white handkerchief in his right hand, the sultan gazes at a lady who kneels at his side on a settee. From his moustache to his baggy pink trousers, he is dressed as the consummate foreigner, contrasting with the lady in French gown and elaborate coiffure. The sultan is on the point of asking her to waltz.

During the high period of Delft Blue ceramics, 1640–1740, a popular form was the flower vase. The Dutch loved flowers and so did Princess Mary, daughter of James II of England, who in 1677, at the age of fifteen, married her first cousin William of Orange. Mary's pastime was collecting Chinese porcelain and Dutch delftware. The Dutch East India Company imported flower bulbs and porcelain, and the royal couple commissioned Dutch and Flemish artists to create delftware for their palaces. A popular design was the bust of a turbaned Turk, which accounts for the name of an important Rococo Dutch factory, the Young Moor's Head Factory. An early eighteenth-century turban bust in the Kunstmuseum den Haag is knotted to one side, made to serve as a flower-holder. It has seven holes in the head and on both shoulders. Pyramid-shaped flower vases also included holes and spouts for individual blossoms. Figural designs on flower-holders included putti as well as Moorish figures and other men with turbans.

A Meissen group dated 1747 presents the trope of a male servant offering a lady coffee on a tray. A young black man at the left and a white courtier on the right flank the woman, possibly a princess, who sits on a gilded chair. The lady ignores the bewigged courtier, who presses his body against her voluminous skirt, and turns her face to regard the other man, who is dressed in a multicoloured Oriental costume with a white turban that shows off his ebony skin. Like the turban, the lady's face and hair are whitest porcelain. The black figure acts out an Orientalist *pas de deux*, answering the European's every wish. The black figure is not enslaved; he might be of high office, a prince of a faraway kingdom. In figurines of this sort the 'princess' has an equal, romantically, in the foreigner, whether a servant boy or a pasha.

When tobacco reached Europe in about 1500, smoking quickly gained a reputation for manliness and honour. Handcrafted pipes

Turkish head pipe bowl carved out of meerschaum, 1800s.

soon became available in Holland, England and elsewhere in Europe. Some were of kaolin, but wooden pipes with bowls of walnut, clay and porcelain became popular in the eighteenth century. Some had metal caps or decorative chains. Advances in printing technology meant that whole scenes of reproductions of painted figures could be transferred to porcelain pipes. Of all the materials, however, meerschaum (German for 'sea foam', which it resembles) was the most prized. Sculpted of a soft white stone from Turkey and Africa, the design enjoyed the greatest hold on pipe-smokers' imaginations. Many such pipes were carved in Austria, but since the stone was from Turkey it was natural that Turks' heads be carved on them. The turbaned head often appears in the centre of the bowl, the turban fitting into the shape of the pipe.

In 1724, five years after his novel *Robinson Crusoe* (an early international best-seller), Daniel Defoe published *Roxana: The Fortunate Mistress*. As the British Empire expanded, Orientalism became more popular, and the heroine Roxana, above other literary creatures, exploited the glamour of the Turkish harem. Of Huguenot parentage and English-educated, she traded her charms for fortune. At a masquerade party Roxana is holding in her home, she realizes that a king – readers are not informed which king – is among the guests in their various disguises. While the men dance a measured *danse à*

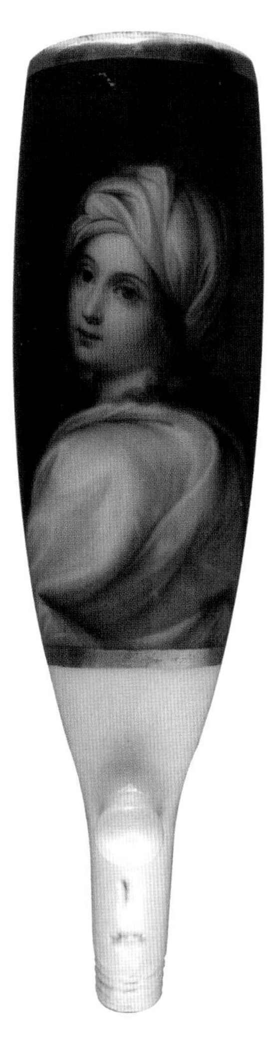

Porcelain tobacco pipe with a small cauldron, 1830–50.

la comique, she retires from the party and returns dressed as a Turkish concubine in authentic clothing bought in Livorno. Her patron there had brought her a servant, who not only helped her to shop for these 'cloaths', which had reached the markets of the Italian port city, but showed her how to dress in the unfamiliar garments. The 'cloaths' include 'Persian or India Damask Robes' and a turban with a pinnacle 12 centimetres (5 in.) tall and with a piece of 'loose sarcenet' (a heavy silk) hanging from it at the front, just over the forehead. Roxana embellishes the turban with a 'good jewel'. She is elated to have purchased the outfit at 60 gold coins (Spanish *pistoles*), a lower price than it would have fetched in Turkey.

English masqueraders of the eighteenth century impersonated Persians and Turks because of their romantic association with exotic luxury. Putting on a dancing-girl costume is an overtly sexual act that removes Roxana from the strictures of her presumed European morality. Dancing as a harem beauty frees her to conduct exciting seductions. She declares that she never expected to wear the costume at a gathering, 'tho' I had dress'd myself in it many times, by the help of my little Turk'. To don the unfamiliar diaphanous garment and turban required know-how. In her silk robe, turban and jewels, Roxana is revealed to be of false character (even though the book is written in the first person). At the macabre end of the novel one of her abandoned children turns up, now a teenager. She recognizes her mother as a woman who wears Turkish clothes and conducts 'lude' entertainment. The daughter wants to blackmail her. Roxana's maid pays off the daughter before dragging her away and having her murdered. Roxana couldn't care less. In festivals and at balls in the eighteenth century, being disguised in costume violated decorum and subverted class and sexual boundaries.

After graduating from the University of Cambridge and before buckling down to government posts, John Montagu, the 4th Earl of Sandwich, embarked on private travels. The portrait and genre painter Joseph Highmore painted him at the age of twenty in costume, looking gangly and with a sparkle in his eyes. He wears a furred green robe, a bright red tunic and a pink turban with a jaunty knot, a spiffy get-up. The earl did indeed give his name to the humble and ubiquitous two slices of bread with filling in between. One story goes that hunger could not pull the inveterate gambler away from the card table. Instead, Sandwich would call for meat between two slices of bread. His colleagues, equally passionate gamblers, followed suit with 'Bring me whatever Sandwich is having.' His name was also given to the Hawaiian Islands by Captain James Cook, whose explorations the earl promoted.

Our interest in the earl goes back to his undergraduate life at Trinity College, Cambridge, where the classical world engaged him. He was a good student, especially of Greek and Latin, and his reading of a long poem about the Phoenicians set his sights on the Classical world. This interest moved him to extend his Grand Tour in 1737 to Greece, at the time rarely explored by aristocratic travellers. Extraordinarily, he pushed on to Turkey, where he spent several months as documented by Liotard.

Back in England, Sandwich founded a dining club for people who had visited or planned to visit the sultan's dominions. The Divan Club lasted for only two years, 1744 to 1746, but its members published scholarly books of their travels and included politicians, such as Sir Francis Dashwood – whose portrait shows him jolly with a ruby embellishing his turban, and a tall glass of red wine in his right hand – and clergymen, among whom was Richard Pococke, Bishop of Ossory in Ireland. Like the other members of the club, Dashwood and Pococke liked to drink and discuss the archaeology and cultures of the countries they had visited.

Lady Mary Wortley Montagu was in her early fifties when the club was formed, living in Avignon, but her voluminous correspondence, written while accompanying her husband, Edward Wortley Montagu, to the Ottoman court, was honoured in the club's official toast, 'The Harem!' Her flurry of letters, and their posthumous publication in

1769, delighted her many correspondents with detailed descriptions of the lives of Turkish women, especially in the *hammam* (bathhouse). In her correspondence, Lady Mary chided her readers' stereotype of Turkish women as slaves to their husbands. Rather, she averred, Turkish women enjoyed more freedom than their English counterparts because of their right to own property and to divorce and, provocatively, to enjoy one another's company in the bathhouse in the nude. In a long description she compares the Turks' ease with

W. Greatbatch after C. F. Zincke, *Lady Mary Wortley Montagu*, 1844, engraving.

their bodies to herself removing the stays in her riding outfit, to the delight of the women bathers she visited. Lady Mary was also famous for entertaining and for posing for portraits in Turkish dress – so famous, in fact, that in addition to the authentic portraits, anonymous portraits of women dressed *à la turque* were often said to be of her. The publication of her correspondence gave a large readership an intimate understanding of the lives of women previously hidden from view.

As for the Divan Club, the only written record of the society was a minute-book called Al-Koran, but memoirs, collections and portraits of some of the 25 members in Turkish dress have survived. It is likely that they wore costumes to the dinners, for this was a dining club (catered for at the cost of a crown a head), Sandwich was its 'sheik' and wearing a turban was the norm. Pococke wrote to his mother as he journeyed to the East that he would soon be 'in the Turkish habit, a turban and all'. And it was customary for the club's members to sit for their portraits in Oriental dress. Liotard received commissions to do Turkish-costumed portraits of at least five members. A life-size painting of Pococke shows him dressed as an official in the sultan's court. 'The costumes depicted were always of the most luxurious nature,' the historian Rachel Finnegan observes, 'signifying wealth on the part of the sitter as well as an eagerness to emulate the most powerful citizens in the east.'[13] Some members commissioned Liotard to make portraits of their wives and mistresses in Oriental dress several years after the Divan Club closed its doors.

The spirit of Orientalism as an abstracted type suffused portraiture. Over the course of the eighteenth century, wigs gradually became outmoded for men. Instead, they smoked in dressing gowns with their heads wrapped in turbans. Wrapping one's head in textile manifested leisure generally, a misty dream of being an indolent Middle Eastern potentate. Joseph Wright of Derby was best known for his 'candlelight' paintings of the mid-1760s, his depictions of scientific and engineering processes, and his self-portraits at ten-year intervals from the age of twenty. Mostly he chose to show himself in a turban, and the fabrics and the jaunty way he wore them demonstrated that he tied a turban well. A painting from 1765–8 in the National Gallery of Victoria, Australia, shows him in pensive mood and evokes Rembrandt. His chin rests on his right hand and his turban, of silvery cloth with thick white metallic stripes, must have been his dress-up best. The artist's daughter Harriet Wright packed the painting in her belongings when she emigrated to Australia on a small cargo ship with her nephew John Edward Cade and two of his daughters.

Wright repeatedly painted himself in a turban, while John Singleton Copley brought the vogue for Turquerie into portrait painting in America. He painted the cream of society in the decade before the American War of Independence, when, in common with certain upper-class Englishmen, some urbane Americans were wearing turbans – presumably not only when sitting for their portraits, since they

Left: John Singleton Copley, *Ebenezer Storer*, c. 1767–9, pastel on laid paper mounted on canvas.

Right: John Singleton Copley, *Nathaniel Hurd*, c. 1765, oil on canvas.

John Singleton Copley, *Nicholas Boylston*, 1767, oil on canvas.

look too comfortable for that to be the case. The turbans in Copley's portraits no longer betoken cultural difference; instead, the affluent colonial Americans who commissioned him were advertising a sense of adventure and a connection to an emerging world economy. An establishment American was unlikely to have made a Grand Tour to Turkey, but he may have made sea voyages of equivalent distance.

The first time Copley painted Nathaniel Hurd of Boston, in about 1765, he showed the silversmith and engraver in his work clothes. Hurd gave his creative energies to his craft, so his head-covering, the turban, is a focal point. A portrait of Nicholas Boylston (1767) has more luxuriant and pronounced details that fall into the category of Turquerie. Boylston sits at ease in a green Persian dressing gown known as a *banyan* (Gujarati for 'merchant'). A colonial person in hot, humid Virginia might have worn a lightweight banyan in public but Boylston, whose family's fortune derived from sugar plantations worked by enslaved Africans, lived in Boston. His silk pink-red turban attests to his elite status. Whatever work he did on behalf of his international dealings did not interfere with his everyday leisure.

Copley also painted American women wearing turbans. The idea of the seraglio came to America with the publication of the letters of Lady Mary Wortley Montagu. The headdress she saw in a harem she described as 'composed of a cap . . . fixed on one side of the head, hanging a little way down with a gold tassel, and bound on, either with a circle of diamonds . . . or a rich embroidered handkerchief . . . The hair hangs at its full length behind, divided into tresses braided with pearl or ribbon, which is always in great quantity.'[14] According to the British art historian Marcia Pointon, colonial women were drawn to Turquerie because they loved the clothes, which represented a 'feminized sexuality'.[15]

In Copley's portrait of Margaret Kemble Gage (1771), her turban has a tassel and is complemented by a long, flowing gown. At first glance, New Jersey-born Gage is representing herself as up-to-the-minute fashionable, ratifying her connection to London society and reflecting the authority of her husband, General Thomas Gage, who led the British troops in Massachusetts at the beginning of the Revolution. On further inspection, however, her prominent turban seems an expression of her strong will and her secrets despite her husband's prominence, she spied for the American cause. Was it a prop in her wardrobe, or had it belonged to her father, who had lived in Smyrna (now İzmir), Turkey, as a boy? Whatever the circumstances, Copley has painted her in a mood of reverie; she may be present, but her thoughts are far away. One of the last of Copley's turbaned ladies, Abigail Smith Babcock, a shipowner's wife from New Haven, Connecticut, painted circa 1774, wears a dress open in the front with a low neckline and full white sleeves. She has a turban of gauzy silk, worthy of a pasha; it doesn't cover her brown hair but sits high back from the forehead. Like Gage she looks, if not placid, removed from the world.

Thomas Jefferson, the United States' most European president, may have brought to America the first painting of a turban. For five years, 1784–9, he lived in Paris and proved a classic cultural tourist who enjoyed French food so much that he sent his enslaved young cook to cuisine school. He purchased furniture, kitchen equipment and art for his rented residence, appropriate to his position as American ambassador to the court of Versailles. These purchases of fine furniture, paintings and sculptures, which he later shipped home in eighty crates, would grace Monticello after his presidential term (1801–9). Mostly he admired Old Masters, although he singled out for praise *The Death of Socrates* (1787) by his contemporary Jacques-Louis David.

At an auction Jefferson bought a copy of a painting by the early seventeenth-century artist Guido Reni entitled *Salome Bearing the Head of St John the Baptist*. An earlier title of the painting, *Herodias*, was misleading because, according to the Gospels of Matthew and Mark, Herodias was the mother of the girl who danced for Herod, not the girl herself. Although now notorious as Salome, in the New

Unknown artist, after Guido Reni, *Salome Bearing the Head of St John the Baptist*, after 1692, oil on canvas.

Testament she is nameless, just the daughter of Herodias. (The Jewish historian Josephus gave the daughter her famous name in the first century CE.) The two Gospel stories relate that Herodias, Herod's wife and an avowed enemy of John the Baptist, arranged for her daughter to dance at the birthday party of King Herod, her stepfather. The dance was so well received that Herod told the girl he would give her whatever she wished, even half the kingdom. After consulting with her mother, the girl asked for the head of John the Baptist on a platter. Reluctantly, Herod ordered John beheaded, and the head was delivered to the daughter.

In the sixteenth and seventeenth centuries several leading artists tackled the subject of Salome holding the head of John the Baptist. All the paintings contrast the youthful beauty of Salome and the gruesome head. Antonio de Solario presents her with jewels in her

Angelica Kauffman, *Self-Portrait*, 1784, oil on canvas.

hair. Titian gives her a plumed hat. Jefferson's copy depicts her with a turban, silk and padded, and decorated with a brooch of pearls and gems – a young aristocrat with a taste for the Turkish East. She gazes straight ahead, presenting the head to the viewer, a promise fulfilled.

The painting hangs at Monticello on the upper tier of the parlour. Since it depicts a biblical scene, it recalls Jefferson's version of the Christian Bible, which he composed by selecting only those verses that taught moral values. Jefferson cut and pasted this version when he retired to Monticello in 1809, and did not intend it for publication. Miracles such as the Virgin birth and the Resurrection of Christ are absent, but it includes the story of Herod and the dancing stepdaughter who forced the king to execute the radical John the Baptist. Jefferson entertained frequently, so it is reasonable to assume that conversation among his guests turned occasionally to the painting of the young woman wearing a turban.

In the eighteenth century, history paintings were a high form of art in which Angelica Kauffman, a child prodigy born in Switzerland and trained in Italy, had a stellar career. Her turbans covered the heads of major biblical and classical figures – women as well as men – and in her themes she played with cross-dressing. She and her husband, Antonio Zucchi (who spared her from household concerns so that she could concentrate on her art), lived well in Rome and were friends with such figures as Johann Wolfgang von Goethe and Joshua Reynolds.

In one of Kauffman's paintings set in Classical times, *Achilles Discovered by Ulysses among the Attendants of Deidamia* (1769), Achilles receives a bad omen about the imminent war with the Trojans, so he hides on the island of Skyros and cross-dresses with a group of women to avoid being taken off to fight. Odysseus, king of Ithaca, learns from a prophet that without Achilles he cannot win the war against the Trojans. Odysseus visits the court of Deidamia disguised as a peddler of women's clothes and jewellery. He tricks Achilles by showing the group of women a shining sword nestled among the feminine wares.

Achilles reaches for it, revealing that (s)he is a warrior just as Kauffman is the artist wielding the paintbrush, thus subverting the normative triangle of male painter/male patron/female sitter. Odysseus wears the robe and turban of an Ottoman, in a sense his own disguise as a non-Greek.

Over a long career, Kauffman painted more women wearing turbans than did any artist before her time. Some were generic, others specific people. An example of the former is *Morning Amusement* (*c.* 1784), in which the sitter is dressed in a satin robe, two gossamer chemises, pantaloons, slippers and a turban tucked on the sides to reveal her hair. In the privacy of her room, she embroiders. The painting was reproduced mechanically and distributed widely as a print. In another history painting about the Trojan War, *Hector Taking Leave of Andromache* (1768), Hector wears a distinctive Greek helmet, but his wife and her servant wear gold-embroidered rolled turbans. The turbans hint at the fate of Hector, who will die in battle in Troy, across the strait in Asia. In *The Return of Telemachus* (1773), Penelope and her attendants wear turbans stylishly propped on the back of their heads, leaving their hair visible. When Odysseus does return, Kauffman does not portray the scene of his self-revelation to his wife. Rather, in *Penelope Awakened by Eurycleia with the News of Ulysses' Return* (1772), she paints Penelope in a deep sleep dreaming about her absent husband. Penelope and her servant Eurycleia, who have cannily defended their home during Odysseus's long absence, wear turbans.

In a portrait by Kauffman of an actual person, Mary, 3rd Duchess of Richmond wears a sumptuous fur-lined robe and gold-brocaded chemise, pantaloons, velvet slippers and a rolled turban tied loosely towards the back of her head so that her hair frames her face. Alongside lies her embroidery frame, and she holds in her lap a roll of finished work. Seven years before this picture, the duchess dressed as 'Fatima the Fair Sultana' at a masked ball at the London Opera House in honour of the visiting Danish king Christian VII. At the ball, many wore Turkish costumes especially notable for the baggy pantaloons

Johan Joseph Zoffany, *Queen Charlotte with Her Two Eldest Sons*, 1764, oil on canvas.

and svelte turbans. Sappho is turbaned in one painting, and Queen Charlotte in another. A patron of Kauffman, Margaret Bingham, in her portrait wears a gold turban high on her head and holds open an atlas.

In England, William Hogarth – arguably the first great political and moral satirist in Europe – looked at turban-bearers with irony. The artist did not let slave-owners and their habits go unscathed. In his *Taste in High Life* (1746), a frivolous company of upper-class Londoners gather in an opulent sitting room. One, pictured as a monkey, reads a French menu. A woman holds up her own dress train while she chucks her black pageboy under the chin. The page himself is painted as an element of irony who mocks the fashion victims. His turban has a bunch of feathers, and he has a pearl earring and metal collar. The convention whereby an enslaved person looks adoringly at their owner is humorously observed. Hogarth also painted a high government official, Sir Robert Pye, seated in a relaxed pose, legs crossed, in his garden folly. Sir Robert looks sporty in a silk turban that matches his long jacket.

The 'big hair' and tall feathers of the 1770s characterized big turbans festooned with flowers, crêpe, foil, pearls, cut steel gems and feathers, worn by the likes of Jane Austen and Dido Belle on ordinary occasions and also at fancy-dress balls. English fashion plates show plumes – two, three or even more – that stood straight up from the turban and curled slightly at the top ends. The turbans could be white or coloured, and sometimes ties jutted out. As hair was dressed closer to the head at the end of the 1790s, turbans followed suit. Austen called this a cap, although it was also sometimes called a bonnet or turban. These female turbans were light, of such material as muslin, crêpe or taffeta, sometimes fringed, and ranged from wrapped cloth to more structural forms. Ringlets peeked out from underneath, and additional bandeaux could be stitched on to wrapped turbans, some of which had an end hanging over the shoulder in what was intended to be a Turkish look.

In France and elsewhere, new fashions followed the French Revolution. By 1790 the new, vaguely Eastern 'confederation turban', which became known as the Phrygian or liberty cap, with a conical shape and curled front, briefly symbolized the new republic. Cropped hair and a turban, being very far removed from the elaborate wigs of the Bourbon women, was a safe look. Not only Empress Joséphine, but many other democratic patriots of Europe brought variety to their chemise dresses with shawls and turbans. In 1795, newspapers offered guides on how to match a turban with the rest of one's toilette. The look was soft hair and soft turban, as evidenced in the self-portrait of Marie Antoinette's portraitist, Élisabeth Louise Vigée Le Brun. The most striking finery of a Regency or Empire belle was on her head. Ostentatious and high-positioned women appeared in a rather grotesque display of ostrich feathers, and a jewelled stick pin or brooch at the front of a turban often matched their dresses. More was more, and made good copy in the fashion news. For example, hand-painted aquatints published in English fashion magazines, such as the *Gallery of Fashion*, between 1794 and 1822 showed headdresses *à la turque* that competed with one another to be both peculiar and brilliant. They have such an assemblage of dyed heron and ostrich feathers that they look as though the ladies' heads are bending under their weight. They are worn over short hair or an updo, often with a coiffe drawn tightly through the turban in ringlets; or the fringed ends of the turbans fluttered to the waist. One silver gauze turban was paired with a silver-trimmed muslin gown with silver sash and yellow shoes. There are large, jewelled pins, some in the shape of diamond stars, at the crown of these turbans. A scarlet and white ensemble has matching ostrich feathers on a turban constructed from a spotted taffeta scarf. Another aquatint has a coquelicot (bright red) crêpe turban matching a dress.

Following the *Gallery of Fashion* into the twentieth century, the Sitwells were a prominent English literary family. Sacheverell Sitwell also collected books, including an almost complete set of the *Gallery of Fashion* plates, which he deemed 'the greatest of all coloured costume books'.[16] His sister Edith, an eccentric dresser, was one of the most famous turban-wearers in England after the First World War. She bobbed her hair in the 1920s, but continued to wear wafty long skirts, often of brocade, and extravagant headdresses. The wife of a cousin described her as 'dressed in black with a chintz pinafore and wearing a red turban'. On Edith's mother's side the family genealogy went back to the Tudors, leading the older brother Osbert to quip that headdresses and brocade decorated by semi-precious stones were appropriate to his sister's '"Plantagenet" head and figure'.[17]

Dame Edith sat for her portrait numerous times. In Paris, at a soirée held by the novelist and art collector Gertrude Stein, she met

Isaac Cruikshank, *Gallery of Fashion*, 23 March 1796, hand-coloured etching.

Russian artist Pavel Tchelitchew, who painted her six times. One of these portraits shows her in mauve, with a red turban on her green and gold hair. The English painter Wyndham Lewis worked for more than a decade, 1923–35, on a portrait of Edith that is now in the collection of the Tate. In this portrait her eyes are almost closed beneath an olive-green turban, and the artist left out her hands. By the time the work was completed Lewis was a recluse who explained that he had come to dislike Dame Edith for being so keen on publicity. In her later years, she wore voluminous dresses and abundant necklaces and bracelets with her turbans.

A twenty-first-century version of Dame Edith appears in a series of colourful and edgy photos by Tim Walker, taken in 2008 and published in *W* magazine. Actress Tilda Swinton poses as Dame Edith at Renishaw Hall in Derbyshire, the Sitwell ancestral home. The actress wears turbans composed of a Marc Jacobs belt and a Gucci hood. In one photograph she lies in a bed of anemones and wears a zany high turban by Michael Kors. In another image Swinton poses in a brocaded turquoise dress and black velvet stacked turban.

In this chapter we noted Queen Anne's darkened skin, a form of blackface, an appropriation with which few today would agree. In enslaving African people, Europeans and Americans committed an extreme appropriation of bodies. The playful use of black skin in masquerades and theatre was an extension of slavery and racial injustice. John Locke called for protection from 'turbanned nations', but he remained mostly silent about slavery. We also discussed the place of Zamor, enslaved, in the court of Louis xv. Cultural appropriation, such as of clothes, food, poetry and lifestyle, does not remove the object from another's ownership. Rather, it is an imitation, sometimes closely resembling the original, sometimes fanciful. Some of it may offend twenty-first-century taste, but in their day the borrowers found beauty and delight. The appropriateness of the imitation was and is a matter of taste. Slavery is different, a matter of basic human rights.

Other forms of appropriation checker Middle Eastern attempts at modernization. When the Ottoman Turks occupied Constantinople in 1453, they tolerated the Christian community as a continuing population but established sumptuary regulations to constrain who wore what. Usually these regulations attempted to restrain extravagance of clothing or ornamentation. They also publicly marked out minority religious communities. Christians were required to wear white turbans and Jews were constrained to wear yellow, for example. These rules varied over time but held until the early nineteenth century, when Napoleon's invasion of Egypt and defeat of the Mamluks spurred the Ottoman sultan Selim iii to create a new army wearing European uniforms, including hats, and bearing European arms, meaning rifles. The tight-knit infantry of the Janissaries refused to cooperate with the new army. Backed by the *ulema* (Muslim scholars) and other elite groups, the Janissaries revolted and deposed the sultan. As a defence of their traditional clothing, they cited the Hadith, 'The turban is the barrier separating belief and unbelief.'

That Selim's reform failed did not arrest the efforts of the Ottoman leaders to regain their traditional military strength against the Europeans, especially European communities within the empire who pushed for independent nation status. When the next sultan, Mahmud II, likewise moved to create a modern army, again the Janissaries revolted, but the sultan was strong enough to suppress and in a short time annihilate them. This launched a series of changes, including dress reform. Most Turks replaced turbans with fezzes, and robes with jackets and trousers. Officially, turbans were for the heads of the Muslim clergy and Sufi mystics only. Following traditional wisdom that the people follow the ways of the kings, by the end of the nineteenth century Muslim men in countries from India to South Africa wore the fez as part of their religious identity.

Muslims pray by prostrating themselves and touching their foreheads to the floor or ground. To do this, they do not take off their turbans. The fez reform of the 1830s did not alter this ritual. In the aftermath of the First World War, Mustafa Kemal Atatürk overthrew the Ottomans, abolished the Caliphate and created an explicitly secular, anti-clerical government. As part of this, in the sumptuary tradition of the Ottoman past, he ordered male Turks to wear brimmed hats instead of fezzes. The brimmed hats were unsuited to prostration. This did not stop men from praying, but it did underscore Atatürk's insistence that Islam and modernization were incompatible. For the time being, Muslim clergy and Sufis retained the right to wear turbans, but in 1934 Atatürk forbade the clergy from wearing turbans outside their houses of worship. This limitation holds to the present day.

The Qajars, a Turkish people, invaded Iran from their homeland in the Caucasus region to the west of the Caspian Sea in the late eighteenth century. Their second ruler, Fath Ali Shah, created a centralized government and, like contemporary Ottoman sultans, introduced European military dress. He also introduced the kolah, a tall black lambskin hat, as the necessary headdress of subsequent Qajar shahs and high government officials. Other Iranians could wear hats or turbans as they wished. Sufis and clergy continued to wear turbans. During the Qajar period (1794–1925), the kolah completely replaced the turbans favoured by Safavid kings.

Appropriation leaps to our attention when it demeans another culture or when a misunderstanding flares up that injures one or both parties. An example of the latter occurred in Iran in 1907. In 1897 the Qajar government invited a Belgian, Joseph Naus, to lead a reform of the government's treasury and customs. This was part of an overall effort to modernize the bureaucracy. In 1907 Naus attended a masquerade party dressed as a cleric, complete with white turban. A photo of him circulated widely, causing offence because he was wearing the garments of an Islamic scholar. When a leading cleric, Ayatollah Behbahani, saw the image, he took to the pulpit and pronounced that Naus had 'mocked Muslims' and 'broken the back of Islam'. The cleric requested that Muhammad Ali Shah charge the Belgian with treason and expel him. The shah resisted because Naus had improved tax and custom revenues for the government, but the public interpreted the masquerade as making light of their religion, Shia Islam, and in the end the king sent the Belgian home.

When Reza Shah Pahlavi, a modern secularist like Atatürk, took over the government in 1925, he pushed men to wear brimmed hats and even prohibited women from wearing veils. Like Atatürk, he assumed that religion should play a smaller, more private part in the life of a modern state, and that dressing alike would give the various peoples and ethnic groups that inhabited Iran a stronger sense of national identity. His son, Muhammad Reza Shah Pahlavi (r. 1941–79), continued the Westernization of women's dress in Iran. His second wife, Farah, shopped for clothes regularly in Europe and the United States. During the shah's rule, most urban Iranian women completed high school, and many entered the country's training centres and universities and adopted Western dress.

Modernists who launched the 1979 revolution that sent the shah into exile soon gave way to traditional Shia clergy who wear turbans as an official headdress. Although this clerical government has attempted to roll back the Westernization of women's clothing, it has left civilian men, in both urban and rural areas, to their own choice of clothing. Iranian heads of state and *mujtahids* (legal authorities) join the Saudis and some of the rulers of the Gulf States as the only current national leaders to wear turbans.

Paul Emile Detouche, *Scheherazade*, 19th century, oil on canvas.

5

Riding the Magic Carpet

In the literature of the Baroque period, writers dressed the 'Orient' in a romantic glamour of proto-Orientalism. Classicists were alarmed by the import of culture and ideas from the East – 'The barbarian is at the gates!' – but no one could resist the fascination of the international story corpus called *The Arabian Nights* (or *The Thousand and One Nights*), and its 'Once there was, once there was not' entertainment. In the frame story, Shahzeman (or Shahzaman), the king of Samarkand, visits his older brother Shahriyar, the king of China and India, and relates the discovery of his wife in bed with a slave; Shahriyar murders the pair. The next day Shahriyar invites his brother to hunt, to console him in his grief. Shahzeman declines, and while his brother's party is out hunting, he espies Shahriyar's wife cavorting with a slave. When Shahriyar returns, Shahzeman advises him to go out on a hunt but to return during the day, so that he can see for himself. Shahriyar follows the plan, and kills his wife and her lover on the spot.

The bad fortune confronting these kings is understood to come from a powerful realm of slaves, as well as from the opposite sex, whose perfidy lurks beneath their beauty. Henceforth, Shahriyar doubles down and every night sleeps with a virgin before murdering her. Three years of revenge pass, and the king's vizier can no longer find an eligible woman. When the vizier's oldest daughter,

Shahrazad, learns that her father is in trouble, she offers herself. But, since she is learned and has read a thousand history books, she prefaces sex with the king with a story, which she leaves incomplete. Then follows a postcoital promise to complete the story the next night. Thus she lives to continue the tale; on the next night, she launches a new tale. Each night she leaves the king in anticipation. Story-telling frames the sex. The king's sexual satisfaction does not end his need for her. After one thousand and one nights she asks the king a favour: may she see her two children by him? The king grants her wish, renounces his policy of revenge and marries the storyteller to his brother.

The enormous popularity of *The Arabian Nights* in the Muslim world and then in the West attests to its strange power of beginning a story, branching off mid-story to a new story, and branching again until it returns to its point of departure. What the reader and King Shahriyar learn is that life is not a series of one-night stands.

In 1704 the French Orientalist Antoine Galland wrote in a preface to his translation of these stories that 'you need only read them to agree that we've never seen anything of this kind, in any language, of such beauty.' He published the translated stories serially; a crowd would gather before his house and throw stones up to his window, clamouring for the next episode.

Readers are to imagine the costumage, but turbans surface to be part of the plot itself. 'The Third Kalandar's Tale' is a concatenated tale that begins in the same way as the biblical episode of Jonah and the Whale. A prince is sailing in a ship when the captain loses his reckoning during a storm. He sends the lookout man up to the masthead. The man spies something dark, like a huge fish floating before them. When the captain hears the lookout's words, he dashes his *turband* (Galland's version of the word) on to the deck, plucks out his beard and beats his face. They are shipwrecked by Magnet Mountain because it attracts the nails in the ship, but the prince has a dream that eventually leads him out of danger.

One of the more erotic scenes occurs in 'The Tale of Nur Al-Din Ali and Son'. The Lady of Beauty strips and the man's desire is aroused. He removes his *turband* and puts it on a settee with his clothes, remaining in only his skullcap and blue silk shirt. The couple embrace and, to complete his pleasure, the Lady is a virgin.

In Richard Burton's explanatory notes for 'A Lady and Her Five Suitors', he makes the claim that this witty tale 'over-wandered the world', including having a presence in Indian folklore and Italian literature. (Giovanni Boccaccio was fond of the device of trunks and cabinets.) In the version of *The Arabian Nights* that Burton translated, a clever woman tricks five well-off men in order to steal their fine clothes. She is a merchant's daughter whose husband is a great traveller. He sets out for a distant country and is absent for so long that

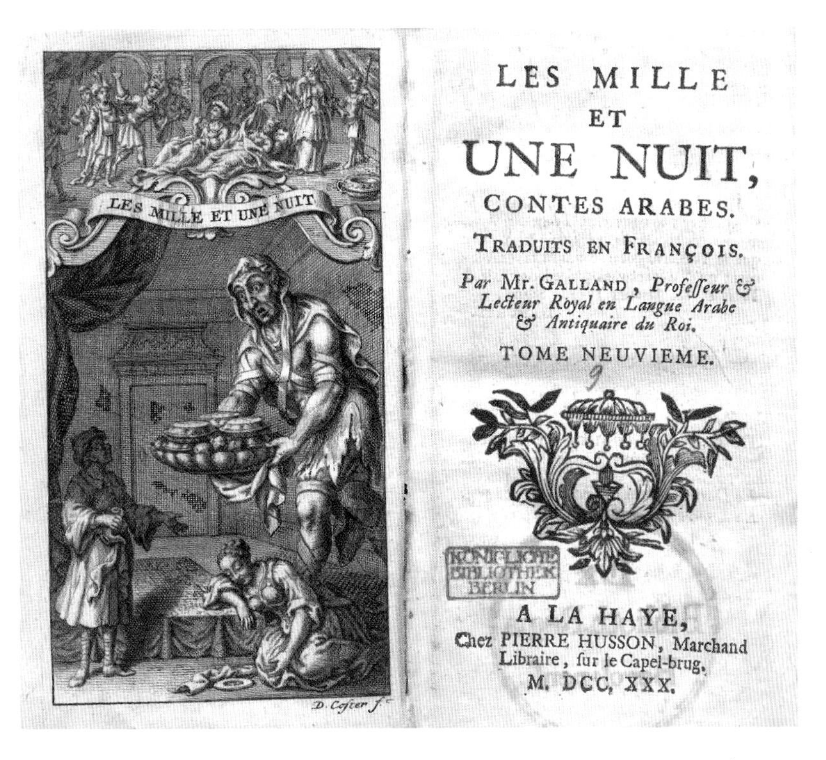
LES MILLE ET UNE NUIT

LES MILLE
ET
UNE NUIT,
CONTES ARABES.
TRADUITS EN FRANÇOIS.
Par MR. GALLAND, *Professeur & Lecteur Royal en Langue Arabe & Antiquaire du Roi.*
TOME NEUVIEME.

A LA HAYE,
Chez PIERRE HUSSON, Marchand Libraire, sur le Capel-brug,
M. DCC. XXX.

A French edition of *Les Mille et une nuit* (The Thousand and One Nights) by scholar and traveller Antoine Galland, whose translation was published in twelve volumes, 1704–12.

from ennui his wife falls in love with a handsome merchant's son. When this young man is imprisoned, she goes to the chief of police, claiming the man, whom she calls her brother, has been imprisoned wrongfully. The chief takes a fancy to her and she invites him to her house for a whole day to rest before they make love. Then she goes to the *kazi* (judge) and asks him to intercede with the chief of police. The *kazi*, too, wants her to come to his house, but she tells him that her house has slave girls. Then she goes to the vizier and even to the king of the city. The king hears her story and his heart is pierced with love, but she declines his invitation by telling him that he will do her more honour by coming to her house.

On her way home, the merchant's daughter orders a carpenter to make a special cabinet. It must have four compartments, one above the other, each with a door locking it up. When she asks what the price will be, the carpenter says he will make it and then 'come to thee at my leisure'. She now takes four gowns and dyes them each a different colour, after which she applies herself to making ready meat and drink, fruit, flowers and perfumes. She anoints herself with perfume and spreads her sitting room with rich carpets to await the four men.

The *kazi* appears first. She jests and toys with him, but when he wants sex, she says,

> 'Oh my lord, doff thy clothes and turband and assume this yellow cassock and this head-kerchief, whilst I bring thee meat and drink; and after thou shalt win thy will.' So saying, she takes off his clothes and turband and dresses him in the cassock and kerchief. But hardly has she done this, when lo! there comes a knocking at the door.
>
> 'Who is that rapping at the door?' asks the *kazi*.
>
> 'My husband', she replies.
>
> 'What is to be done, and where shall I go?'
>
> 'Fear nothing, I will hide thee in this cabinet,' she says, and he tells her, 'Do as seemeth good to thee.'[1]

Each of the men is secured without food or drink in the cabinet, which is small for them, and eventually one pisses on the other. These rich officials of the city are now in 'queer disguises', which they have soiled. As a merchant's daughter she knows the value of their fine clothes, which she takes to run away with her lover.

This rather short story is visually vivid. The four prosperous men come into the merchant's daughter's house dressed for romance in fine clothes. They expect she will cede her body to them because they are people of authority. Thus their robes and their turbans also belong in the narrative picture of the story, contrasting with how ridiculous they look at the tale's end.

A collection of Turkish fairy tales has turbans as a common device. In 'The Magic Turban, the Magic Whip and the Magic Carpet', two brothers receive an inheritance from their father. The profligate younger one is always begging for money from the elder, who has bought a shop. Seeing his profits disappear in this manner, the elder brother sells his business and sails to Egypt as a merchant. Meanwhile the younger one stows away on board the ship. When the younger is discovered, the elder brother says, 'Stay there and I'll go and get mules to carry us further.' Instead, he departs on a magical adventure, gathering violets as he goes, until he comes to the foot of a mountain where three men quarrel over who gets a magic carpet, whip and turban their father bequeathed to them. The elder brother tricks them into running after an arrow, and while they are occupied he rides off on the magic carpet, wearing the magic turban, which renders him invisible. The carpet takes him to the sultan's castle. The sultan is beside himself because his daughter disappears each night. The merchant flies to the bedroom of the princess and follows her out at night to the castle of the jinn (spirit) who has bewitched her. There awaits sherbet in diamond-studded cups, but the merchant spoils the repast and severs the jinn's head. The sultan demands an explanation of the goings-on . . . or off with the merchant's head. The elder calls for the younger brother, who speaks up for him and reassures the sultan that his elder brother is trustworthy. Asking nothing for himself – since he knows that with the magic turban, carpet and whip he can always earn a living – the elder brother persuades the sultan to give his daughter's hand in marriage and half the kingdom to the younger brother. He now wants to remain near the brother he once tried to flee.

The princess, released from the spell, has only abhorrence for the jinn and agrees to marry the younger brother. Their wedding festivities last forty days and forty nights. The storyteller of this typically witty and piquant fairy tale concludes: 'I was there also, and when I asked for pilaf, the Cook gave me such a blow on my hand that it has been lame ever since.'[2]

A large corpus of humorous, often satirical, short tales attaches to the popular character Mulla Nasreddin.[3] Anecdotes about how witty and wise he was have altered and stayed alive as they have travelled from his birthplace in Konya, Turkey, throughout the Islamic world. One of the stories comes from the corpus of tales that eventually comprised the *Arabian Nights*.[4] In a Turkish version, the story takes place during Ramadan, the Muslim month during which the pious observe abstinence from the first light of dawn to the onset of sunset (Qur'an 2:187).[5]

Nasreddin is working in the field ploughing and sowing wheat. As the sun dips towards the western horizon, he realizes the hour is getting late and he ought to go home to wash and put on clothes appropriate for the evening feast at his wealthy neighbour's. He says to himself, 'Is it better to be late, or a little dusty? And besides, I haven't eaten all day.' So he decides to join the breakfast celebration dusty and in working clothes. Brushing himself off, he goes to his neighbour's house and knocks on the door.

When the host opens the door and Nasreddin enters and begins a conversation with one of the other guests, that person looks through him as though he is invisible. The same lack of acknowledgement follows with two other guests, so Nasreddin goes quietly home, washes and puts on a beautiful robe and cotton turban of many folds. When he returns to the party he finds himself the centre of the festivities, and the host asks Nasreddin to sit beside him.

Food is served, and Nasreddin takes a *kofta* (meatball), which he slips into the pocket of his robe. Then *dolma* (stuffed vine leaves) are brought in, and he takes a couple and conceals them up his sleeve. When olives are offered, he stuffs several into a fold of his turban. The amazed host asks, 'Nasreddin, why do you put food in your robe and turban?' Nasreddin replies, 'When I came in my work clothes and still dusty, no one paid me any attention. When I appeared in my fine robe and turban, everyone greeted and welcomed me. It must be the robe and turban who have been invited, not me. Therefore I am feeding them.'

The turban has a starring role in one of the most famous Middle Eastern tales of all, from the historical province of Khorasan in north-eastern Iran. Hans Christian Andersen's version is 'The Emperor's New Clothes', in which a silly king is tricked to preen with nothing on and becomes a laughing stock among his people. The story made the journey to Europe from the wisdom literature of India, whence it was transmitted to Khorasan as 'The Invisible Turban'. In this version, there is no fool and the king is smarter and less gullible. An apprentice dervish writes a short poem that pleases the king, who gives him a reward. Then the dervish recites a much longer poem, expecting a bigger reward, but the king is in a terrible mood and orders the dervish executed. To save his life, the dervish promises to weave an imaginary turban that only people of legitimate birth can see. The king gives him money for the necessary materials and a house outside the city to complete the task. Meanwhile the dervish prays fervently for a way out of his predicament.

The king sends a messenger to visit the workshop where the textile is being woven. The dervish puts on a show and raves about the design and brilliant hues of the fabric he is weaving. The messenger, who sees nothing, commends the dervish because he is afraid that otherwise he himself might be exposed as of illegitimate birth. The messenger returns to the palace and praises the cloth to the king's vizier. When the vizier goes to see for himself, the dervish holds up the 'cloth', and the vizier admires it.

When the time comes for the dervish to present the cloth at court, the king asks him to describe it. But the king, who sees nothing, orders that the vizier's mother be brought, and accuses her of having engaged in sexual contact that has hexed him. The lady denies it and the king threatens to execute the vizier unless he reveals the truth. The dervish confesses all, from his decision to impress the king with poetry to his stratagem of proposing to weave the imaginary turban to save his life. The king forgives the dervish but decides to punish the vizier. Summoning his courtiers, he turns to the vizier and says, 'Instead of wearing this turban myself I prefer to see it every day on you.' With that the king orders the dervish to place the turban on the vizier's head. The vizier shivers, the king explodes in laughter and the vizier is disgraced. The king makes the wily dervish his new vizier.[6]

The main source of non-Muslim slaves for the Abbasids (750–1258) were young Turkish men from lands to the north of Iraq and Syria. They were converted to Islam, learned Arabic and trained in the military arts. In Egypt this cadre became so powerful that in the thirteenth century they took over the rule of that country and parts of Arabia and Syria. They were known as the Mamluks, the 'owned', because of their origin as slaves. The presence of fair-skinned young men in a society that severely restricted casual relations between unmarried men and women led to the practice of homosexual relations between older Muslim men and young Turkish boys. One of the most famous poets of the Abbasid period, Abū Nuwās, wrote explicitly about his sexual relations with these boys. By the time of the Mamluk Empire (1250–1517), it was an accepted topic, usually treated ambivalently but sometimes licentiously.

Mamluk Egypt produced many distinguished writers and poets, one of whom was Khalīl ibn Aybak al-Ṣafadī. Al-Ṣafadī, who hailed from Safad in present-day Iraq, held important government posts in different cities in the Mamluk territory during the fourteenth century. One of his most widely read books, *The Plaint of the Lovelorn* (*c.* 1350), takes up the infatuation of an adult man with a Turkish boy. The poem is not licentious, in that it concentrates on the awkward flirtation that leads up to a night of sexual embrace. Most of the poem describes the endless tears the man sheds while the two are separated between liaisons. In their second meeting in a Cairo garden, the Turkish youth, a soldier, proposes that they skip the sweet talk and retire to the lover's home. A friend of the lover orders a banquet, and after carousing, they fondle and kiss. But before they consummate their relationship, the youth asks the man, 'By God, do you incline more towards this one, or towards singing slave girls?' The lover replies, 'If love of Salma is better for one's life, and passion for Nu'ma is more delightful for one's eye, I have nevertheless contented myself – with a beloved in a turban.' Discretion holds to the end, when the narrator of the poem asks about the sex: 'Generous time gave us a wonderful night/ But do not ask what happened between us.'[7]

Important forms of literary expression in Arabic, Turkish and Persian literature highlight wit and wiles. An example comes from the thirteenth-century *Book of Charlatans* by Jamāl al-Dīn ʿAbd al-Raḥ īm al-Jawbarī, a collection of witty sayings and events. In it a sheik astonishes his neighbours when he walks home from the mosque, his head blazing with golden light. When he sits in the mosque and lights up its dark corners, the faithful leave him coins. But his head inside the turban begins to itch. He squirms and forty glow-worms he had woven into a hairnet are revealed.[8]

In the burst of book illustration from the late nineteenth to the mid-twentieth century, Charles James Folkard rode the wave. Born in south London in 1878, he created Teddy Tail, a cartoon mouse, and was renowned for colour-plate illustrations for editions of *The Swiss Family Robinson* (1910), *Pinocchio* (1911) and *Grimm's Fairy Tales* (also 1911). Folkard had a flair for composing magical scenes. As a child he designed

Illustration by Charles James Folkard in *Ottoman Wonder Tales* (1915).

programmes for his own magic shows, and before illustrating story collections including *The Arabian Nights* (1913) and *Ottoman Wonder Tales* (1915) he was a professional conjurer. In these publications the trappings and setting are inspired by old Persian manuscripts. While the story characters are rosy-faced English schoolchildren at play in Western popular culture and children's books, turbans have a magical cast instead of signifying identity, rank or religion. Nursemaids who served the Bourbon court told action-packed romantic stories to their aristocratic charges. High-ranking ladies developed the rustic stories

Illustration from *Histoire du Prince Ardelin* (1779).

into worldly *contes*. Thus one anonymous mother, in an anonymous collection, amused and instructed her three young daughters with a story that starred an exotic prince, Ardelin, which was published with watercolour illustrations.

In Rudyard Kipling's novel *Kim*, published in 1901, the protagonist is a vagabond orphan, the son of an Irish soldier and an Indian nursemaid. As an orphan, Kim identifies with the many ethnicities of India. A 'Hindu kit' allows him to pass as a low-caste boy or a Brahmin or a Muslim. Because he is white enough to pass as a *sahib*, a British master, and dark enough to fit into the flow of indigenous Indian life, he is conscripted into a British spy network hidden within the Survey of India led by Colonel Creighton. In addition to his training in mapping and working with rods and other surveying equipment, he learns spying techniques in the curio shop of Lurgan Sahib, all to give Kim the skills he will need to assist the British in the Great Game of preventing Russia gaining easy access through Afghanistan to the Indian subcontinent.

The training involves a ten-day Jewel Game in which Kim and an uneducated Hindu boy attached to Lurgan must memorize a large number of objects. These Lurgan selects from his inventory of such oddities as the ghost daggers with which Tibetan exorcists stab demons, devil masks, peacock-blue draperies, Persian water jugs, carpets, firearms and jewels galore. Kim, who at the opening of the novel frequents the Lahore Museum, declares that the museum is indeed larger than Lurgan's shop, but that the shop has more wonders. At the end of the each day, Lurgan tests their memory of the objects and the objects' features.

When the Jewel Game training is complete, as a reward, Kim and the other student play dress-up in a shop with 'all manner of turbans'. The variety of fabrics is such that Kim dresses as 'a young Muslim of good family, an oilman, and once – which was a joyous evening – as the son of an Oudh . . . in full dress'. (Oudh was the British name for Uttar Pradesh in northern India.) He 'enjoyed himself too much to reflect on the craziness' – crazy because the variety of turbans allows Kim to mimic the variety of religious affiliations, castes and social classes populating the subcontinent.

In Lurgan's shop, the two boys also sit out of sight and observe the many people who enter. These customers include government clerks (*babus*), minor rajas, women with and without veils, low castes as well as high, Hindus and Muslims. At the end of the day, Lurgan again questions the two boys on what they have learned. What Lurgan learns is that Kim is a master mimic who delights the master spy with his imitations.

Kim learns to identify people by their turbans: a maharaja wears a tight turban; an inhabitant of Peshawar wears a gold-embroidered turban with its cap rising to a cone and a big turban cloth ending in a broad fringe of gold. In pursuing his career as a spy, he applies his skills in 'hot and crowded bazars' or on the Grand Trunk Road, 'the backbone for all Hind . . . a river of life as nowhere else exists in the world'. The film *Kim* (1950; dir. Victor Saville), starring Dean Stockwell in the title role, was filmed on location in northern India. Turbans abound on the heads of many castes and several religions, bringing to cinema audiences the turban as a nationalist rather than religious marker. The film includes the famous scene in Lurgan's shop where Kim identifies the various turbans Lurgan is selling by region and caste as well as by religion. As we will see in Chapter Seven, a famous display of a turban was on the head of a Hindu, Vivekananda, at the Chicago Exposition in 1893.

Joseph Wood, *Dolley Madison*, 1817, oil on canvas.

6

A Neoclassical Accessory

While enslaved women were wearing headwraps in the Caribbean and North America, there was a parallel influence of fashionable garments *à la turque* during the Napoleonic period in Europe. Although Napoleon's invasion of Egypt (1798–9) is most famous for the investigation and description of ancient Egyptian buildings and art, the brief occupation also contributed to contemporary French fashion. When he returned to France, Napoleon included Mamluk soldiers in his personal guard. His favourite, Rostand, appeared in his pre-eminent white turban on a Sèvres china cup and saucer celebrating Napoleon's imperial ambitions. As Napoleon conquered more nations, his soldiers sported uniforms highlighted by flamboyant headgear. Only once, while in Egypt, did Napoleon himself attempt a Mamluk uniform. According to a memoir by his friend Louis-Antoine Fauvelet de Bourrienne, 'The General cut such a poor figure in his turban and caftan; he looked so gauche and self-conscious in that unfamiliar garb, that he soon left the room to take it off and never felt tempted to repeat the masquerade.'[1]

Before becoming Napoleon's first wife, Joséphine was a socialite and trendsetter, and wife of Alexandre Marie, vicomte de Beauharnais. An aristocrat and royal officer, Alexandre was executed as a traitor during the Revolution. Joséphine was scheduled for the guillotine the next day. She cropped her hair short to ensure that it would not become entangled in the instrument's blade. Joséphine owed her life to her friend Thérèse Cabarrus, a decade older, whom Robespierre nearly sent to the guillotine. Thérèse and Joséphine met when they were imprisoned in the Carmes Prison, a converted monastery, in Paris. Joséphine wrote with her own hand a poignant message on a windowpane and countersigned by Thérèse: 'Liberty, when will you stop being a vain word? We have been locked up for 17 days. They tell us we will be out tomorrow but isn't this a vain hope?'[2]

The representative of the governing convention in the city, Jean-Lambert Tallien, fell in love with Thérèse, who, with one day to spare, was able to save Joséphine from the guillotine. When married to Napoleon, Joséphine amplified her styles to match his triumphs, and as part of the Egyptian craze when he returned from Egypt she formally donned a turban. Joséphine may have wrapped a turban around her head when in jail, to protect her short coiffure. During the Directory, in 1797, the first Ottoman ambassador since 1742 came to Paris. He was received with fanfare, and for a season dressmakers were flooded with orders for robes *à la turque* and turbans. Thérèse set the fashion. In a cameo from 1798 she looks every inch Neoclassical in her thin chemise, yellow draped shawl, and turban weighed down by her hair at the back of her head.

Napoleon's favourite sister, eleven years younger, was the intractable, pretty Pauline Bonaparte. A clothes horse, she favoured the Neoclassical languid look and is depicted with the simple hairstyle *à la creole*, which Joséphine also wore. Pauline was the wife of General Charles Leclerc when Napoleon sent him to San Domingo (now Haiti) to quell the Haitian revolution. She was reluctant to go to the West Indies, but was persuaded by her friend Laure Permon, the wife of General Junot, another military officer close to Napoleon. Knowing what appealed to her friend, Laure suggested how fine Pauline would look in a turban: '"You really think, Laurette", she inquired, "that I shall look pretty – prettier than usual – in a Creole turban, a short waist and a petticoat of striped muslin?"' Young Madame Junot straightway contrived from scarves and bandanas a passible imitation of the exotic costume of the Antilles. Pauline dressed herself in them, looked at herself in a mirror and was completely delighted. In his memoirs, Prince Metternich, who got to know Pauline when he was the Austrian ambassador to France, wrote that she was 'as handsome as it is possible to be; she was in love with herself, and her only occupation was pleasure.'[3]

The military expedition to San Domingo was disastrous, but Pauline thrived as a social butterfly. She claimed to those back home, 'Here I reign like Joséphine.' A member of the expedition's squadron remembered her as a 'Maritime Venus'. Her personal staff commonly dressed in Hussar tunics, with yellow pantaloons, striped stockings and Mamluk-style plumed turbans. Pauline adopted features of the local manner and dress of women of colour. She dressed in a muslin morning gown with a madras (a strong cotton fabric) head-kerchief. She wore outfits of a new vogue at the consular court: a low-cut dress with full skirt and train called the *robe à la Psyché*, influenced by the island costume. Leonora Sansay, an early woman novelist of the American Federal period, published an epistolary novel set in Haiti that was based on letters she had written to Aaron Burr before he served as Thomas Jefferson's vice president in 1801–5. Sansay described Pauline as 'rendered interesting by an air of languor which spreads itself over her whole frame', and noted the 'Madras handkerchief on her head'.[4] Pauline shocked a member of the general's staff when she attended a traditional Creole dance, presumably joining in. The reception at the commander's house was called an 'appointment in a death house' because many seemed to catch their death there. Such was the case with her husband, the general. After he died of yellow fever, she returned to Paris, pregnant and with her embalmed husband. She lived in Italy for the remainder of her short life, dying in 1825 at the age of 44.

British fashions followed the French as a rule, although the nomenclature was different. Jane Austen wore a turban with a plume for an evening out. In 1799 she wrote to her elder sister, Cassandra:

> I am not to wear my white satin cap tonight, after all;
> I am to wear a mamalone [Mameluke] cap instead which
> Charles Fowle sent to Mary, and which she loans me.
> It is all the fashion now; worn at the opera and by Lady
> Mildmays at Hackwood balls. I hate describing such things,
> and I dare say you will be able to guess what it is like.[5]

The fashion press recorded with exactitude what ladies at balls attended by royalty wore. The turbans matched the Neoclassical dresses and were festooned with jewels and feathers.

According to fashion historian Hope Greenberg, turbans and other headwear in England and on the Continent followed hairstyles. By the end of the century, hair was dressed closer to the head, and turbans were snug. As hats became smaller around 1805, Greenberg notes a shift from wrapped turbans (a long length of fabric wrapped around the head) to diminutive hat-like things that were called turban caps, or if they were wrapped on a cap, turban caps.[6]

'Mamalone' was Austen's rendering of 'Mamluk' or 'Mamalouc', and the cap was a turban, often decorated with plumes. The mamalone turban could be white or coloured, and sometimes ties jutted out from it.[7] In the Romantic era, a brief fashion of the *nouveau riche* was the '*turban de fantasie*' that swelled and rose in spirals. This youthful turban took its name from E.T.A. Hoffmann's collection of stories known as *Phantasiestücke* (Fantasy Pieces; 1814–15). As usual, the upper class's role was to stay ahead of the bourgeoisie. Paris and London traded styles back and forth, and colourful turbans were often accessorized with an aigrette and a jewel. A *coiffeur* would create a turban that matched one's coat. For evenings, turbans featured an ostrich or peacock feather.

Born a Quaker, First Lady Dolley Madison adhered to plain clothes in her youth. She married James Madison in 1794. In her new role as wife of a prominent politician – he was a Virginia representative to Congress – she had a keen eye on European fashions and soon adopted turbans as her signature accessory. For Madison's presidential inauguration, she wore a buff velvet dress with short, puffed sleeves in the Neoclassical style, and a turban to match, decorated with bird-of-paradise feathers.[8] As First Lady, her favourite material for turbans was white velvet, but she also wore blue and red ones, often with ornaments.

In 1813 Dolley wrote to her friend Elizabeth Patterson Bonaparte, wife of Napoleon's brother Jérôme, asking her to look for a 'turban, or even anything brilliant to make me [*sic*] such as gauze or lace flower'd with gold or silver'.[9] In 1816, at a reception for the wife of the British minister Charles Bagot, Dolley wanted to dazzle the guests in the wake of the war of 1812. She wore a white velvet turban trimmed with ostrich tips, and a gold-embroidered crown. One can imagine petite Dolley, head held high, as her personal maid, Sukey from the Madison farm in Virginia, helped her to dress. In formal portraits, Dolley wore other styles of turban in rolled fabric, sometimes fastened to a straw cap and other times wrapped directly on her head. In daguerreotypes from the 1840s she wears a simple white wrap of silk. The painter Thomas Sully portrayed her contemporary Sarah Reeve Ladson Gilmor of Baltimore in a Byronesque multicoloured silk turban with a tail hanging to her left and a bow fastened above her right ear. She wears an Oriental robe over a Late Empire décolletage.[10]

In the 1830s, after being a professor at Harvard for two years, Henry Wadsworth Longfellow sought a better boarding house in which to reside. He saw a beautiful house on Brattle Street with a view of the Charles River, and enquired about a room. The landlady, Elizabeth Craigie, a widow, turned him away because she didn't take Harvard students. 'I remember how she looked as she stood, in her white turban, with her hands crossed behind her, snapping her grey eyes,' he recalled. The turban by now was somewhat outdated from its pre-revolutionary vogue, but it gave the widow authority. Notwithstanding the initial rebuke, the poet made so bold as to present himself as Professor Longfellow. It turned out she had read one of his books, which was lying on a nearby table – a sketchbook describing his travels in her beloved homeland, France. Widow Craigie showed him the rooms, and he and later his family lived in the house the rest of his life.[11]

Under the pseudonym Vicomte Delaunay, Delphine de Girardin wrote a weekly column in which she chronicled daily *mœurs* in France during the rule of Louis-Philippe (1830–48). In 1837, when leaving a ball in Paris, she noted a mode for all kinds of turbans that year: those of heavy gold fabric, and light ones of lace, gauze and tulle. According to Girardin, now was the time 'to burnish one's turban, to have one that swells and rises up in folds, just like whipping cream, of the sort that Mlle de Beaudrant was admired for wearing: a young turban, a turban of fantasy'. However, the ultimate foolishness (*niaiserie*) was to suppose that such a fashion would attract men who might say, 'Madame! How well the turban becomes you, you look like a beautiful odalisque.' 'To the contrary,' the commentator said, 'those women who wore extravagant versions of turbans could expect to be derided.'[12]

Madame de Staël, née Anne-Louise-Germaine Necker, was known as a turban-wearer. Contemporaries remarked of her 'enormous turban' that it was a way of presenting herself 'as the sultana of thought'. Evidence of Necker's ability to stand out in a crowd goes back at least to her introduction to the French court at Versailles. Two weeks after she married the Swedish ambassador Baron Erik Staël von Holstein, she made her debut at court. She arrived late and began the ceremonial three curtsies. Upon the third, she was to kneel before the queen and kiss the hem of her dress. But as Germaine knelt, she tripped on the train of her gown, lost her balance and fell flat on the floor.

One of the most famous French women of her time, de Staël was outspoken in her liberal politics and held friendships with many luminaries of the era, including Thomas Jefferson, Lord Byron, the Marquis de Talleyrand, Lord Wellington and William Wilberforce. Napoleon hated her, and the feeling was mutual, since she opposed his tyrannical aim of absolute rule. For this she was exiled on and off during his regime. Napoleon quipped that she should attend to her knitting, but she never did. Her final political activity, from 1814 until her death in 1817, was to assist in abolishing the slave trade.

De Staël dressed as she wished. Adam Geczy writes in *Fashion and Orientalism* (2013), 'It seems that de Staël's turban was her own improvised equivalent of what the banyan came to be for men.'[13] Let it not be said that men are repelled by an intellectual woman, since she had scores of admirers. Or that a homely woman was jealous of a beautiful one; her best female friend was the goddess of the day, Juliette Récamier. De Staël in several portraits wore a round style of turban, twisted from two colours of silk. In one portrait, beneath the turban, she wore a wide band of jewels in a Neoclassical look, covering part of her forehead, thus connecting a symbol of Eastern wisdom with the headband on Classical sculptures of women.

Why else did de Staël choose this signature style? To be distinctive and to keep her hair neat for her constant social engagements and on long voyages by carriage. Her small round turban suited the short hairstyles, whether the *coiffure à la Titus,* cropped to the back of the neck and with a fringe (named after the son of the Roman conspirator Brutus, a character in a play by Voltaire), or a coiffure called the Psyche knot, hair drawn up at the back, curls over the forehead and ringlets over the ears. De Staël had an array of colourful turbans to choose from. Along with the Indian shawls lavished on Joséphine by Napoleon which became the vogue in the early nineteenth century, turbans in pastel colours brightened the pale chemise dresses inaugurated in the Directory period. The colourful turban with the *à la Titus* hairdo was self-important but consciously distanced from more elaborate hairstyles.

Many who admired de Staël shook their heads at her appearance in middle age. Goethe described her as a superior but awkward spirit (*mal logé*). Caroline Schelling, a German intellectual three years older than de Staël, said her clothes gave her the air of a *vivandière* (a woman who sold provisions to soldiers).[14] Besides wearing the turban, when at home at Coppet, her castle on the shores of Lake Geneva, she also held a little bunch of branches that was renewed each day by her gardener.

The painter Jean-Auguste-Dominique Ingres never travelled to the Middle East, but he did read a French translation of Lady Mary Wortley Montagu's *Letters* and translated her somewhat detached (and accurate) description of the bathhouse (*hammam*) into a series of scenes of nude women relaxing in and by the waters. Working from Jean Baptiste Vanmour's engravings as well as Lady Mary's *Letters*, Ingres made *The Small Bather* (1828), which presents a small group of women at their ease, some nude, some partially covered. At the rear, one woman wears a tall, carefully wrapped blue turban; in the middle of the room, another bathes in the nude; and at the front, dominating the painting, one figure looks into the bathhouse, slippers off, wearing a gold and white turban wrapped thickly about the rear of her head. Oriental costumes and accessories in Ingres' art were readily available from Paris shops that purveyed such Eastern goods as 'turbans, striped cotton scarves, fly-whisks and hookahs'.[15] In his late work *Le bain turc* (The Turkish Bath; 1862), Ingres attempts a large bathhouse scene. In the foreground, the frontal woman of the *Small Bather* sits with her back to the viewer, wearing the same gold and white turban as in the earlier painting, and playing a mandolin. The music seems to stir the others to a low-key, voluptuous ecstasy. In their midst sits a blonde having her hair scented. A contemporary French critic opined that this woman was Joséphine Bonaparte's cousin, Aimée Dubucq de Rivéry, whom corsairs captured in 1788 on her way back to France from Martinique and delivered to Sultan Hamid I. According to this critic, Aimée spent the rest of her life in the sultan's seraglio as one of his favourites.[16]

The painter Eugène Delacroix travelled to North Africa in the 1830s after France's invasion of Algeria. Although part of a diplomatic party, he sought to befriend and paint the residents as they were, not as imagined. He sketched more than a hundred scenes of the life of North Africans, including horsemen and their horses, lion hunts and

Jean-Auguste-Dominique Ingres, *The Small Bather*, 1828, oil on canvas.

battle scenes, but to his chagrin he had to take an armed guard when he wandered through the streets of Meknes. In a letter to his friend Jean-Baptiste Pierret, Delacroix wrote:

> As the people here hate the dress and appearance of Christians . . . it's always necessary to be accompanied by soldiers, which didn't prevent two or three quarrels which could have been very nasty because of our position as

Eugène Delacroix, *The Women of Algiers in Their Apartment*, 1834, oil on canvas.

envoys. I am escorted, every time I go out, by an enormous gang of onlookers who heap insults upon me.[17]

Delacroix did gain entrance to some homes of Sephardic Jews in Morocco, and to one Muslim home in Algiers. His painting of the Muslim women, *The Women of Algiers in Their Apartment* (1834), was a sensation in France and frequently copied. In the painting, three women relax on carpets, slipperless and sporting dark turbans sprinkled with gold threads. On the right, an African servant, well-jewelled and wearing a bright orange and yellow turban tied at the front, turns to attend one of the seated women. The servant's turban and matching skirt beautifully balance the ladies of the house.[18] In Tangier, Delacroix attended a Jewish wedding and in an interior apartment sketched women dancing for the bride. In 1841 he turned the sketch into a painting, *Jewish Wedding in Morocco,* which records the white turbans of the musicians and other men, and coloured turbans on a few women seated along the walls. In the Middle East, depending on local custom, minority Jews sometimes wore turbans to blend in to the predominantly Muslim society.[19]

Jean-Léon Gérôme, an artist famous for his classical scenes, took his first trip to Egypt in 1856. Among his companions was Frédéric-Auguste Bartholdi, who designed France's gift to the United States, the Statue of Liberty. On their trip, they undertook a sartorial rite of passage. They dressed in Egyptian cotton robes (*gallabiyah*), Gérôme donning a turban and Bartholdi a fez. Gérôme wrote to his father, 'I had my head shaved and am letting my beard grow; soon I won't be far from looking thoroughly like an Egyptian. I'm dark enough for that.' Recasting himself as a '*peintre ethnographique*', Gérôme took Arabic lessons from Edward Lane and over the next forty years produced several hundred Orientalist pictures. One of the most famous, *Bashi-Bazouk* (1868–9), features a black man dressed in the elegant turban favoured by the Albanian mercenaries employed by the Ottomans to terrorize civilian populations for their recompense in lieu of salaries. Ethnographic it is not; it's a studio piece. In place of a face that inspires fear, Gérôme presents a pensive black man wearing an elaborate turban festooned with tassels and a pink silk tunic highlighted by his dark skin. He is confident rather than desperate.[20]

The English writer Charlotte Brontë gave a blue and silver turban with a feather a part to play between two characters in *Villette,* one of a number of Orientalist images in the novel. The teachers Lucy Snowe and Dr John are at a school concert at which lottery prizes are given:

> Two little girls, of five and six years old, drew the numbers: and the prizes were duly proclaimed from the platform. These prizes were numerous, though of small value. It so fell out that Dr John and I each gained one: mine was a cigar-case, his a lady's head-dress – a most airy sort

> of blue and silver turban, with a streamer of plumage on one side, like a snowy cloud. He was excessively anxious to make an exchange; but I could not be brought to hear reason, and to this day I keep my cigar-case: it serves, when I look at it, to remind me of old times, and one happy evening.
>
> Dr John, for his part, held his turban at arm's length between his finger and thumb, and looked at it with a mixture of reverence and embarrassment highly provocative of laughter. The contemplation over, he was about coolly to deposit the delicate fabric on the ground between his feet; he seemed to have no shadow of an idea of the treatment or stowage it ought to receive: if his mother had not come to the rescue, I think he would finally have crushed it under his arm like an opera-hat; she restored it to the band-box whence it had issued.[21]

Interestingly, Brontë's heroine Jane Eyre compares Rochester to an Oriental despot. Jeffrey Cass has remarked that 'The turban is perhaps the most common metonymy of Victorian Orientalism.'[22]

Nathaniel Hawthorne introduces a turban early in *The House of the Seven Gables*, published in 1851. Once the handsomest house in town, the New Hampshire mansion has been cursed by the first owner, Matthew Maule, whom Colonel Pyncheon accused of witchcraft in the 1690s. In the mania of the times, this accusation led to a trial and the execution of Maule, the colonel's seizure of Maule's property and the construction of the grand gabled house on the appropriated land. Two hundred years later the house is decrepit and occupied by the colonel's great-great-great-grandniece Hepzibah, who clings to the distinguished Pyncheon genealogy but finds herself destitute. To make ends meet, she reopens a former cent store under one of the gables. In her mind, the sale of ordinary goods mocks her status as a

Jean-Léon Gérôme, *Bashi-Bazouk*, 1868–9, oil on canvas.

Pyncheon. The day she opens the store to the busy street that runs before it, she puts on her best clothes, albeit of an earlier era, the 1820s, including a turban of the sort Dolley Madison favoured as French elegance. Echoing the misdeed of Colonel Pyncheon, Hepzibah's cousin, Judge Jaffrey Pyncheon, framed her brother, Clifford, resulting in a prison sentence for a murder he did not commit. When released from prison, Clifford comes to live with his sister. Unexpectedly – and gothically – his cousin the judge dies while sitting in Colonel Pyncheon's chair in the gabled house. This liberates Hepzibah and Clifford from Judge Jaffrey Pinchon's overbearing presence, and the two celebrate by leaving the house, Hepzibah wearing a soft turban similar to that worn by Dolley just before she died in 1849.

In the first two decades of the nineteenth century, Elizabeth Benger and Elizabeth Spence hosted regular gatherings of women writers in London. Benger wrote novels, biographies of royal women such as Anne Boleyn and Mary, Queen of Scots, and a widely read poem on the abolition of the slave trade. Spence wrote travel books and novels that, according to her obituary, inculcated 'morality, religion, and graciousness of manners' in their readers. By invitation only, these gatherings of 'sisters of the quill' included published women writers and celebrities such as Lady Caroline Lamb (briefly one of Byron's lovers) and Sir Edward Bulwer-Lytton, who met and secretly courted Rosina, his wife-to-be – his mother disapproved – at the ladies' events. As hostesses, Benger and Spence often wore turbans. This was appropriate to a more relaxed atmosphere than was found among the classier Blue Stocking gatherings. The ladies' turbans harked back at least a generation and served as a welcome sign to a milieu where women writers could be women. A journalist reported to his wife that at one soirée Spence sported 'a plum pudding sort of turban, with a bird of paradise bobbing over the front'. Rosina reported that at another gathering Spence wore a 'caricature of a turban in gauze and wire'. At the time, the turban lacked status as a public headdress, but the hostesses' literary parties were notable for their devotion to literature and disregard for stylish clothes or tasty food – the fare was dry biscuits and drier sandwiches. Spence remarked to Lady Bulwer-Lytton, 'Our parties, with all their hothouse luxuries (especially the pineapple), quite spoil me for my own, as in my own humble abode . . . I can only pretend to purvey food for the mind.'[23]

Had either lady lived a generation later, she might have decorated her turban with hummingbird feathers, heads or even skins. At the Great Exhibition of 1851, the ornithologist who identified Charles Darwin's finches as species belonging to individual Galápagos islands, John Gould, displayed 1,500 hummingbirds from 320 species, all of them from the Americas. The colours dazzled the visitors and soon the bodies of these smallest of birds became fodder for massive importation as decorations for hats, turbans, necklaces and even little nesters in fur stoles and coats. The supply was so massive that the birds sold for tuppence, and their capture pushed a number of species towards extinction. By the end of the century the Plumage League, a society of women, pledged not to wear any bird feathers on their headdresses.[24]

Charles Dickens featured turbans in some of his Christmas stories. He also supported the career of Elizabeth Gaskell, who wrote popular novels about small-town life. In her *Cranford* (1853), turbans mark the intrusion of foreign threats to the conventions of ladies in the village of the book's title. At the royal top, Adelaide, the German queen to King William IV (r. 1830–37), considered the turban high fashion, a nod to the French, England's arch-enemy during the rule of Napoleon. However, at the time of the story Adelaide is no longer queen, only a memory, much to the relief of the Cranford ladies. One of those ladies, Mrs Forrester, has seen a print of a portrait of Madame de Staël, a prominent supporter of the independence of the American colonies, wearing a turban. This leads Mrs Forrester's friends to discuss contemporary French painters who not only paint Oriental scenes of barely clad harem ladies but, following the example of Madame de Staël, wear turbans themselves.

To reside in Cranford comes Major Jenkins, retired from India, with a turbaned Indian servant in tow. The turban is white – the man is a Sikh – and his skin is brown, an alien of colour. One of the ladies cannot help staring at the servant, both fearful and fascinated. The narrator of the book, Mary Smith, travels often to Drumble, a small industrial city nearby. There the British East India Company supplies clothing shops with turbans. Mary's friend Matty owns a teashop, which is also supplied by the East India Company. Matty associates the Indian servant with Blue Beard in Charles Perrault's tale about a serial wife-murderer, but she would like to add a bit of adventure to her wardrobe by owning a sea-green turban. She requests Mary to buy one in Drumble, but Mary buys a common cap instead. She justifies her substitution: 'I was . . . anxious to prevent her from disfiguring her small gentle mousey face with a great Saracen's head turban.'[25] The Empire notwithstanding, it's just too foreign.

A magician, Signor Brunoni, also comes to Cranford, sporting a beard and turban as part of a Turkish costume. Although a few Cranfordians are sceptical of magic shows, many pay to see him perform. At the end of his performances, the magician accepts an invitation to dine with the locals. Samuel Brown, alias Signor Brunoni, appears without a beard or turban. He is fully English, a retired sergeant. As the novel unfolds, distinctions between foreign and domestic scramble. As Matty's desire for a turban suggests, the headdress is no longer solely Muslim attire, and elements of English fashion are no longer solely European.

Queen Victoria took the title Empress of India in 1877, a few years after the British dissolved the East India Company. As empress, Victoria assumed direct rule over most of the subcontinent. She decided not to attend the Delhi Durbar celebrating her new title. Some 11,250 kilometres (7,000 mi.) removed from India, and without Prince Albert, she was much travelled but felt her age of 58. Instead, she brought to court Indians as servants, initially to handle the Indian princes attending her Golden Jubilee in 1887. Abdul

Christian Albrecht Jensen, *Cathrine Jensen*, 1842–4, oil on canvas.

Karim, a clerk in the Central Jail in Agra, came to the queen's attention when he sent carpets woven by prisoners to an exhibition in London. Karim was educated at home by a tutor and spoke little English. Nevertheless, Victoria invited him to be her orderly. He was 24 and handsome.

En route to England, Karim's transport stopped at Malta. On a tour of Valletta, when an attendant requested that he and his fellow

Muslims remove their turbans before entering an ancient church, they refused and remained outside. In his diary, Karim wrote, 'We could not think of desecrating the sacred building by entering bareheaded.'[26] By the time of the Jubilee, many Britons had seen photographs of and read articles about Indian Muslims wearing turbans, but few had seen them in person. After Karim arrived in London, for most of a week the queen and her guests paraded through London,

Sir William Ross, *Victoria, Princess Royal in Turkish Costume*, 1850, watercolour on ivory mounted on zinc.

giving residents and visitors a good look at the exotic white headdress on the new servant.

Karim taught Victoria Urdu every day, and served her meals. After only a few months at court, he arrived in the royal kitchen with a box of herbs and spices and proceeded to prepare for the queen an Indian meal of curry, dal and pilaf. Victoria loved the food and ordered the kitchen to add Indian fare to its offerings. As we know, immigrants bring their food as well as their clothes.

In the queen's heart, Karim soon replaced her Scottish ghillie, John Brown, a close confidant and constant companion, who had died a few years earlier. The household who managed Victoria's daily life came to resent Karim as much as they had resented Brown. The more the aristocrats at the top of the household complained about Karim's easy access to the queen, the more Victoria defended him. With her steady support, he was transmuted from servant to confidant. Through her influence, he was the first person from India to receive a land grant in his home country, and the first to be included in the queen's meetings and dinners with her extended family and with European royalty. In 1892 the young king and queen of Romania, Ferdinand and Marie (Victoria's granddaughter), met Karim, who, according to sixteen-year-old Marie, stood tall in his white turban and gold jacket, not speaking, while he 'raised one honey-coloured hand to his heart, his lips waiting in Eastern dignity for those things that were to come to pass'.[27]

Because Victoria embraced photography, her court is well documented. Many photos include the stately, turbaned Karim. When Victoria died in January 1901, the complainers found an ally in King Edward VII. A few days after his mother's death, the new king sent his wife, Alexandra, and some guards to Karim's cottage. They demanded from the distraught servant all his letters from Victoria, and burned them. Soon afterwards, Karim and his wife and mother-in-law were summarily dismissed and sent back to India. Except on state visits, never again would the royal residences see a turban in the hallways or curry on the dinner table.

The film *Victoria & Abdul* (2017; dir. Stephen Frears) features Judi Dench and Ali Fazal in the lead roles. That it underplays the damage of colonialism to India provoked controversy. As for costuming, like the sets and acting, it is above reproach. Before Karim goes to England, the governor of Agra sees to it that he is dressed in rich and splendid garments and a big sash. Karim tells him that no Indian wears such a sash, but the governor brushes this away with the comment that it makes him look more authentic. He wears half a dozen different turbans: white striped with red; turquoise-and-khaki-striped plaid; subdued grey; and scintillating white in a tulle-like fabric.

As noted in Chapter Four, in the 1770s–80s John Singleton Copley, an artist with strong ties to England, painted the silversmith Nathaniel Hurd and others in turbans. A generation later, in a nod to European elegance, First Lady Dolley Madison put on a turban for portraits and for special occasions. Officers and seamen who manned America's ships probably saw turbaned men in ports in the Mediterranean Sea and along the coasts of Africa. But few others had seen a turban on a person's head until the World's Columbian Exposition held in Chicago in 1893. Then the audience expanded.

A mere twenty years after the Great Fire had destroyed much of Chicago, the irrepressible metropolis proclaimed its wealth and importance by hosting the Columbian Exposition, which attracted more than 25 million visitors over its six-month run. In those twenty years, the Midwestern city banked a national network of railways, forged iron into steel, built the nation's first skyscrapers with that steel, and turned cattle-farming into the big business of retail meat. The Exposition put on view to millions of guests an array of religious leaders dressed in their distinctive religious garb. As part of the Exposition, Chicago's Christian and Jewish religious leaders hosted the World's Parliament of Religions, which gathered together sixty Confucian, Taoist, Shinto, Hindu, Buddhist, Jain, Zoroastrian and Muslim leaders, as well as Jewish rabbis from Palestine and Christian clergy from Greece and Asia. The Parliament's overall theme, with some dissidence, proclaimed that all religions were from God, that in essence there was one religion in many forms.

Of all the participants, Vivekananda was the star. A member of the nineteenth-century Reform Hindu movement, he wore a sumptuous turban. He delighted many in the audience at the Memorial Art Palace (today the Art Institute of Chicago) by criticizing Christian missionaries, by asserting the East as the source of religious inspiration, and by his devotion to the Hindu mystic Ramakrishna. He was the rhetorical equal to the Chicago Protestants who taught tolerance of other religions on the assumption that with enough interaction they would all join the liberal Christian fold. Vivekananda was also the Protestants' equal in organizing. Before he returned to India in 1895, he established in California and other states Ramakrishna Centers that continue to this day.

Agostino Brunias, *Market Day, Roseau, Dominica*, *c.* 1780, oil on canvas.

7

Individual Expressions: Africa and the Caribbean

As the Muslim community expanded globally in the seventh to tenth centuries CE, Muslim traders and scholars travelled throughout the Muslim world, stopping in ports to trade goods and in cities to seek and impart knowledge. In the eleventh century, the Spanish geographer al-Bakrī questioned visitors to Ghana about their travels, and in his writings he recounted what he learned:

> Among the people who follow the king's religion only he and his heir apparent (who is the son of his sister) may wear sewn clothes. All other people wear robes of cotton, silk or brocade, according to their means. All of them shave their beards, and women shave their heads. The king adorns himself like a woman, wearing necklaces round his head and bracelets on his forearms, and he puts on a high cap decorated with gold and wrapped in a turban of fine cotton.[1]

The Ghanaian king deemed the turban a royal headdress. By the mid-sixteenth century the Portuguese were enslaving Ghanaians and other West Africans and shipping them to their New World colony, Brazil. When Napoleon invaded Portugal in 1807, Prince John and Princess Carlota, along with 10,000 other Portuguese, boarded ships for Brazil. The ships were crowded and moved slowly down the Atlantic to the southern hemisphere. Most passengers were infested with lice. Men threw their wigs into the ocean and women shaved their heads. When they arrived in Salvador, north of Rio, the princess and other royals wore cotton turbans to cover their heads when they disembarked. The local women, most of them enslaved, did not view the royal ladies in the turbans as a surprise, for these people had been wearing turbans since their arrival as enslaved people. The contemporary French artist Jean-Baptiste Debret painted daily life in Rio. Many of his depictions of enslaved women show them wearing turbans, usually in public, selling goods, running errands or celebrating holidays.

As early as the thirteenth century, European aristocrats eagerly sought black African servants, mostly enslaved but some free, for their households. Several passed through Verona around 1240, for example, in the entourage of the Holy Roman Emperor. The iconography of a black attendant to a white European began in the Renaissance, possibly with the artwork of Andrea Mantegna, whose two turbaned Magi are so affecting. An aura of social prestige hovered around the ownership of slaves, despite the fact that slavery was largely absent from the Italian peninsula. In 1491 Isabella d'Este, wife of the Marquis of Mantua and portrayed by Titian wearing a colourful turban of complex design, told her agent in Venice to find her a little girl, '*una moreta*', between the ages of one-and-a-half and four, and 'as black as possible'. When none was readily available, Isabella's mother, the Duchess of Ferrara, hired the whole family of a free black gondolier in Venice, which included such a child.[2]

Benjamin Thompson was a poor schoolmaster who married into wealth in the American colony of Massachusetts as revolution stirred. He gained fame as an inventor, designing a fireplace that delivered more heat and less smoke to its room and house, a boon to well-off homeowners. He was also a Loyalist and spy in the Revolutionary War. After evacuating Boston with the British, Thompson did not return to his wife and baby daughter, although he continued to support them. For his work in helping those who fled the colonies for London, he was knighted. In Munich, where he became Count Rumford and the right-hand man of the Elector, his workhouses sheltered the poor and 'Rumford soup' fed them. He persuaded the Elector to give up his hunting grounds for a public park, which Thompson designed. He successfully implored a foreign general not to burn down Munich during the Napoleonic Wars. For these actions, Munich has a statue of the tall, elegant American on horseback. Thompson was the second most famous American in Europe, after Benjamin Franklin.

Upon his wife's death, Thompson invited his daughter, Sarah ('Sally'), to live with him in London and then Munich, where she was engaged by his cultivated women friends. When Sally returned to America in 1798, she was feted with balls and dressed in fine European apparel, and she corresponded with Countess Mary Nogarola, a close friend of her father. In the last line of a letter, Mary, who was known for her charity and virtue, requested a slave from Sally: 'Don't forget your promise to send me from America a pretty little Negress. Adieu my dear friend – my attachment to you will always exceed that of your Americans. God Bless you! Your affectionate Mary.' The countess desired a slave for decorative purposes. She had servants to freshen up her lemonade or press her linen, but to have an enslaved child follow her around like a pet was a fashion that hid the brutality of the slave trade.[3]

Mary's request probably nonplussed Sally, who, although born into a slave-owning family, objected to slavery. In her later years, Sally commissioned the artist Daniel G. LaMont to paint an imaginary family scene entitled *Benjamin Thompson's Farewell* (1850). Thompson stands out in a red uniform, with sword and tricorne hat at his side. Sally's mother, Sarah, weeps and has a lace mantilla with a small pair of doves perched on her chignon. In the background, the nanny Dinah embraces Sally. The nanny wears a turban that identifies her as a slave, a plain dress as a work uniform, but no slave collar. Sally declared she loved her nanny more than her invalid mother, and credited the nanny with raising her. Her note on the reverse of the painting reads, 'This, of my father taking leave of my Mother, leaving me an infant in the arms of a favourite slave Dinah.'[4]

In the late eighteenth century the Italian artist Agostino Brunias spent years painting in the West Indies. His elegant turbans on working women seem divorced from plantation slavery. He used the word 'servant', not 'slave', and his views emphasized the picturesque. Women, and in one case a man, wear turbans of printed cloth in primary colours. In *Servants Washing a Deer* (*c.* 1775), slaves are washing the master's pet (deer were not native to Dominica). One of the enslaved women is a head domestic in fine clothes: an embroidered skirt, a white blouse with waistcoat, a red-and-gold turban and red slippers.

Elihu Yale, the governor of Fort St George near Madras for the British East India Company, amassed a fortune through extensive private trading, especially in diamonds. His bailiwick included oversight

Agostino Brunias, *A Negroes Dance in the Island of Dominica*, 1779, stipple engraving and hand-coloured etching.

of slave-trading. He returned to London in 1699. In a group portrait, *Eli Yale with Members of His Family and Enslaved Child* (*c.* 1719) attributed to John Verelst, a Dutch artist working in London, Yale sits between his sons-in-law while his grandchildren play in the background. To his left, a young African servant has just poured Madeira into the glasses on the table. He wears a flounced jacket, fancy red and grey livery, and a turban, a portion of which hangs down his back with a pompom at its end. Unlike Sally Thompson's Dinah, he wears a silver padlocked collar around his neck, a standard accessory discouraging slaves from running away. The slave boy highlights both Yale's leisure and his wealth. Yale was a supporter of an Anglican missionary society, which led him to contribute books and money to a new college in the American colony of Connecticut – a college that took his name. His ownership of a slave boy evinces the Church of England's comfort with slavery.

Two cousins figure in a 1778 portrait of Dido Elizabeth Belle Lindsay and Lady Elizabeth Murray by David Martin, which has a cryptic turban. The artist portrays them on the terrace of Kenwood House in Hampstead, north London, at the home of Lady Elizabeth's uncle William Murray, the Earl of Mansfield. The girls appear friends, as the white girl reaches out to Dido to hold her hand. Dido's mother was Maria Belle, an African slave or former slave who was captured from a Spanish vessel in the Caribbean by a British naval officer, Captain John Lindsay. As a small child, in 1766, Dido was sent to England to be raised by Lindsay's uncle the Earl. Lady Elizabeth wears a wreath of rosebuds in her hair. While she is pretty, the viewer's attention goes to the quicksilver girl who is black, whose turban with its jaunty ostrich feather combined with her animated movement suggest a vibrant personality. Whether Dido was treated as an equal or as a poor relation is unknown. However, the career of the Earl of Mansfield was that of a moderate abolitionist. He presided over a case of a runaway slave and ruled that the man could not be taken from Britain by force.

Jean-Baptiste Vanloo, the older brother of Charles-André with whom he decorated the Marquise de Pompadour's boudoir (see Chapter Four), painted Murray in his later years. Five years after the earl's death, Dido, who had a small inheritance, left Kenwood, married a Frenchman named John Davinier and had a family. In the obituary of the earl that appeared in the *London Chronicle,* Dido was described as 'a Mulatto who has been brought up in Lord Mansfield's family almost from her infancy, and whose amiable disposition and accomplishment have earned her the highest respect from all his Lordship's relations and visitants'.[5]

It has been suggested that the painting began as a single portrait and that Dido was added later, a circumstance that would account for the unusual composition, in which she seems to dash forward of her cousin. Mario de Valdes y Cocom, a historian of the African diaspora, proposes that Dido's turban might have been an attempt to Indianize her. In 1770–71, Lindsay served as a Minister Plenipotentiary in India. Naturally the young woman might be wearing a Creole version of a turban; however, Valdes argues that she had not grown up in the West Indies, and that the headgear would be a means of connecting her with her father.

Whether a working adult slave, such as Sally Thompson's nanny, or an essentially decorative child slave as would help Countess Nogarola keep up with her aristocratic peers, the household enslaved were dressed to validate their separateness from white owners. Turbans were part of the facade of gentility, as was the spangled livery worn by the unknown servant boy in the Yale group portrait.

Madras fabric, which was used for turbans and head-ties, was big business for the British East India Company. In the late seventeenth century English weavers rioted over the competition of imported Indian cottons and silks. Some of the unemployed even expressed their grievances by throwing acid over the dresses of ladies travelling in coaches. The Calico Act of 1700 forbade the importation to England of cotton and silk cloth woven in India. The British social reformer

Elizabeth Montagu had to go to the ship in which her brothers sailed from India to bring ashore a gown, probably chintz, which she 'buckled' under her bodice. But the Calico Act did not ban importation to the Atlantic colonies, a growing market. This meant that in the eighteenth century the West Indies enjoyed an ample supply of superior yet affordable cotton and silk cloth direct from India. This was part of the British mercantile policy to limit America and the West Indies colonies to the production of raw materials and keep them open as markets for British finished goods, such as woven cloth.

By 1800 most West Indian headwraps were made from red or yellow checked cotton and produced largely in Europe for the colonial markets. Protective European laws funnelled colonial demand for turbans to their metropolitan industries in London, Paris, Spain and the Netherlands. This included what had for a century been called madras cloth. Linen was also used, but pure cotton was better for holding dyes so that the turban's colours did not fade.

As England and France colonized the Caribbean islands, they brought African people to work the sugar cane, cotton and indigo plantations. Enslaved women brought different kinds of turbans. In Jamaica, the headwrap was called the 'tie-head'. Married women who traded in the markets folded a squared piece of starched madras cloth into a triangle; this was the foundation of a head-covering that was knotted at the back of the head. Two folds of fabric were left to drape to the shoulders or centre back. The upper fold was called the 'cock's tail', which it resembled. To stiffen the fabric to make the peak more pronounced, the women boiled cassava juice to make a starch. In the eighteenth century rebels in the highlands of eastern Jamaica fought the colonial British for their freedom. Women joined the men in combat, and to identify themselves wrapped their heads in identical madras.

In Martinique and Guadeloupe, the headwrap conveyed occupation. Cane-cutter, laundress, nurse, house servant and field worker – each had a distinctive style. The code in St Lucia related to a woman's marital status. According to the St Lucian poet and playwright Derek

Walcott, in the French West Indies turbans played a part in the formal art of flirtation. A certain style could mean that a woman was engaged but might change her mind, or that she might be faithful if she liked you well enough. In Suriname, women tied brightly coloured fabrics together, and the styles had such names as 'Feda let them talk'. For example, a woman might wear a scarf leaving three corners of it loose and sticking out. Each corner apparently represented the human tongue, and the three 'tongues' implied chatter, idle talk or gossiping. An ornate style with loose folds at the ends of the scarf signalled that the woman was about to meet her lover at the corner.

Some turbans of the period of the French Directory and First Empire followed the sophisticated structure of the West Indies. The *tête calendée* had its distinctive fans and diagonal folds, often from a square of plaid madras, with much of the design covered in thick sulphur-yellow paint and pleated in narrow folds over a paper form, frequently tipped over the right eye. The diagonal folding around the head was exact. The arrangement of the ends was the chief opportunity for individual creativity, where two or three corners might be pulled out broadly or rolled tight and pinned until pencil-like.[6]

In the Americas enslaved black people were the basis of the economy for the entire colonial period. Vast numbers of slaves worked the sugar and cotton plantations of the Americas and West Indies, starting in the sixteenth century. Their styles of turbans included headwraps, which were long enough to qualify as turbans, and head-ties. They carried an African heritage, usually single-layered and sometimes called kerchiefs.

Field slaves who worked on the sugar and cotton plantations of the Americas and the West Indies wore a turban or headscarf as protection during hard and long hours of labour. Only a lucky few worked in the homes of plantation masters. South Carolinian Mary Chesnut described the housemaids at Mulberry Plantation on a Sunday afternoon: 'Though glossy black, they were well dressed and were very stylishly gotten up. They were stout, comfortable looking Christians.

The house women, in white aprons and white turbans, were the nicest looking. How Snow White the turbans on their heads appeared!'[7] Cloth sold to slave-owners designated as 'slave cloth', 'Negro cloth' or 'Plantation cloth' was inexpensive and durable. 'Coarse' and 'stout' were the common descriptors, and the turbans must have been either all cotton or a cotton-and-wool blend.[8]

Descriptions of the slaves' articles of dress come from the memoirs of former slaves, plantation-owners' accounts, descriptions by white travellers and advertisements for runaways. Handkerchiefs, many 68–92 centimetres (27–36 in.) square, are often mentioned in these advertisements. For example, the *Virginia Gazette and General Advertiser* in 1799 represented a runaway named Joyce as follows: 'She generally wears a red handkerchief tied round her neck.'[9] An advertisement in the *Norfolk Herald* on 2 April 1801 described a young woman, '16 years of age, tall and likely had on a grey petticoat and a coloured handkerchief tied round her head and no gown on – named NANCEY'.

Attrib. to John Rose, *The Old Plantation*, c. 1785, watercolour on laid paper.

Wrapped headdresses are described as turbans in sources other than the advertisements for runaways. In her much-read *Journal of a Lady of Quality* (1770s), the English traveller Janet Schaw concluded from visiting plantations in the West Indies and North Carolina in 1774–6 that the slaves were happy workers living in stable families. That skewed view aside, she contributed a rare report that 'women had handkerchiefs of gauze or silk, which they wore in the fashion of turbans.'[10] The former slave Louis Hughes recalled in his memoir, *Thirty Years a Slave: From Bondage to Freedom* (1897), that the enslaved women on the Mississippi plantation were given 'two summer dresses and chemises and at least one winter dress, a pair of winter shoes and cloth for a turban'. Hughes's memoir mentions that the owner, a Mr McGee, once purchased red-and-yellow-checked gingham in Memphis to provide 'Sunday only' turbans for the women workers.[11]

The head-coverings seem to have been more prevalent in the African community of South Carolina; fewer headwraps show up in the records of eighteenth-century Virginia. Since handkerchiefs of the period were substantial in size, they could be used for shoulder-coverings or headwear. English and European handkerchiefs were shipped to Africa as part of the international trade in consumer goods; the flat handkerchiefs could then be folded and wrapped in several different styles that resembled turbans.[12] Men as well as women wore the headwraps, as shown in the painting *Music and Dance in Beaufort County* (1785), in the collection of the Abby Aldrich Rockefeller Folk Art Museum in Williamsburg.

Some slaves earned enough to save money for special clothing to wear on Sundays and other festive occasions. The fashions were like music, a means of expression. After their liberation from slavery, black women in the Caribbean and southern United States could reach back to their African roots for elaborate headdresses. Creole women of African descent in the Caribbean islands and in Louisiana and other regions of the American South established a continuity of African heritage in dress. For example, the headwraps of Yoruba women often matched their dresses and were sometimes coloured with indigo dye. In the painting *The Old Plantation* (*c*. 1785), sometimes attributed to the plantation owner John Rose, South Carolina slaves are gathered for Sunday dancing. Several woman are dressed in colourful cotton dresses and striped turbans. The men sport blue and red jackets, possibly wool, and two wear striped turbans. Livery was often imposed on personal manservants. For the men this might consist of coloured doublets and a turban instead of a hat, with earrings and a silver jacket bearing the arms of the owner. Often the plantations raised their own flax, cotton and wool, spun the thread, wove the cloth and made the clothes. George Washington's weaving house was an example of slaves in the late eighteenth century having artisan skills and producing for their masters. A low grade of madras was imported by slave-owners to keep up with the needs of the plantation's enslaved inhabitants.

Louisiana belonged to Spain after the Seven Years War (1756–63) and was governed by Esteban Rodríguez Miró from 1785 to 1791. When a representative of the Holy Inquisition came from Spain to colonial America and declared that he would arrest all infidels, Miró was a voice of reason. He mandated public Catholic observances but did not allow the Church to examine personal belief, thereby preventing the investigation of heresy. The governor, whose name is found (as 'Mero') on New Orleans place and street names today, found the city chaotic to govern, as had the French, and devised city ordinances to bring peace. To help maintain order, his code banned slave dances in public squares on holy days and Sundays until after church. He prohibited gambling, forbade the renting of property to enslaved people, and outlawed the selling of alcohol to indigenous and enslaved people, among other restrictions.

The tignon came to the West Indies and the American colonies with enslaved Africans and, after the abolition of slavery, with indentured servants. It was a variation on the chignon, a knot or coil arranged at the back of the head, derived from *tortillon*, French for twist. Several

François Beaucourt, *Haitian Woman*, 1786, oil on canvas.

François Fleischbein, *A Free Woman of Colour*, 1837, oil on canvas.

kerchiefs of fine cambric or muslin were twisted around it for the aesthetic effect as much as to protect the wearer from the elements. Afro-Creole women of the West Indies and New Orleans developed the tignon to convey information. One elaborate style with peaks had the wonderful name 'Tête en l'Air' (Head in the Air).

One section of the ordinance, the Tignon Law (1786), was designed to reduce the allure of free women of colour, Creoles, who dressed elegantly, with braids and bejewelled hairstyles, and so were perceived as competing for male attention with white women of higher station. The law required Creoles to dress in a manner befitting their subordinate status. Specifically, they were ordered not to wear feathers in or curl their hair, but to comb it flat and cover it with the large plaid kerchiefs, the tignons, that enslaved women wore. Any free woman of colour who wore fine dresses, jewellery and hairstyles would be punished. Miró's thinking was also that these women could not have got such finery – beautiful dresses, bonnets and jewels – except by illegitimate means. The law insulted the Creole women, implying they were idle or prostitutes who gave excessive attention to dress.

The oppressive measure backfired. The New Orleanians loved to dress up, and were unfazed by the sumptuary law. The tignon, explains the writer and artist Carolyn Morrow Long, 'Instead of being considered a badge of dishonour . . . became a fashion statement. The idea was to create an underclass. However, the bright reds, blues, and yellows of the scarves, and the imaginative wrapping techniques employed by their wearers, are said to have enhanced the beauty of the women of colour.'[13] Free women of colour tied their colourful scarves in expressive wrappings. The cloth ends were tied into knots close to the head. Tignons might also boast jewels or other stylish decorations. The bow could be tied at the side of the head, to distinguish a headwrap from a practical head-covering. Some of the cotton patchwork and handwoven striped madras was dyed in Rouen, France, from where it was traded by the English and Dutch East India companies, often made very fashionable with the women's gems, pearls and trinkets.

When President Thomas Jefferson purchased Louisiana in 1803, the Tignon Law expired, but many women of south Louisiana continued to wear headwraps of showy printed fabric. In the 1820s Marie Laveau, an Afro-Creole known to successive generations as the 'Voudou Queen', was New Orleans's most celebrated practitioner of voodoo. A neighbour told an interviewer from the Louisiana Works Progress Administration that Laveau 'always wore a tignon and her dress was like the Creoles wore then. It was a skirt and long loose shirt, tied round the waist with strings . . . She was friendly with everybody, white and coloured, and she walked very proud like a society lady.'[14] One of many Creole businesswomen of her time, she set up shop as a hairdresser, and among her skills was that of wrapping a tignon. Thanks to her outreach to the poor and sick, she was admired and beloved, and the information and gossip she garnered from her hairdressing clientele allowed her to extend her insights to personal counselling. While there is no portrait of Laveau made during her lifetime, biographers agree that her attributes as a voodoo priestess included a shawl, a snake, a rooster, a feather, a magic (*gris-gris*) bag and a turban knotted in seven knots over her high forehead, a signature costume of voodoo practitioners. Her status as queen of the voodoo community and her charitable works made her nationally famous. Upon her death in 1881, the *New York Times* published an obituary.

Funerals were of outstanding importance in Creole culture. People of African descent formed burial societies whereby, in return for a small monthly fee, they were assured of a distinguished funeral. The Dames de la Poussinière wore black hats, while the Dames aux Tignon wore black silk headscarves. In the mid-nineteenth century women of African descent had their portraits painted. Typically the clothes were subdued while the tignon was eye-catching, for example, the yellow tignon of the anonymous sitter in *Free Woman of Colour* (1837) by François Fleischbein. The elaborately tied tignon is high on the woman's head, and curly locks peek out at the sides and back.

About twenty years after the Emancipation Act in the United States, the characterization of black women as symbols of servitude returned in a bizarre twist. In 1889 a minstrel stereotype of the happy-go-lucky black female house slave, in checked dress, white apron and a headwrap covering her hair, was plucked by a flour company to be a racial advertising motif for its self-raising pancake mix. Three different women, the third a white actress of Italian descent in blackface, toured the country performing the slave 'mammy' into the 1950s. Aunt Jemima was awarded a medal for her showmanship at the Chicago Exposition in 1893, when she flipped pancakes in front of a huge crowd. An Aunt Jemima radio show ran from 1930 to 1942. Aunt Jemima dolls, salt-and-pepper shakers and other paraphernalia increasingly viewed as racist were phased out in the 1960s.

In his memoir *Aké: The Years of Childhood* (1981), the Nobel prize-winner Wole Soyinka describes his life in a Yoruba town during the Second World War. He recounts the story of a women's group that assembled to help young brides take on family responsibilities. It was mostly talk until the young wives began complaining about the abusive tactics of tax officers, who confiscated food and other products the women were bringing to the town's market. This awareness energized the group to act: 'The women rose in a body. Hands flew to heads and off came the head-ties unfurling in the air like hundreds of banners. The head-ties flew downwards, turned into sashes and arced around waists to be secured with grim decisiveness.'[15] The women marched to confront and place under virtual house arrest the local chief until he agreed that 'Enough is enough!' During the sit-in, the British District Officer was relieved of his duties and the heavy taxation of women's work ceased. During the course of these weeks, women from the region collected in the town and the protest became a celebration.

Historically among the Yoruba people of Nigeria, brides wore the turban, then a narrow bandeau of cloth. Over time women added more and more cloth to their turbans, which were called *geles* (pronounced 'gayla'), and introduced new methods of draping it. The headwrap has different names in different regions of contemporary West Africa. For instance, in Malawi and Ghana the term is *dhuku*, and in Nigeria it is *gele*. The Tonga people wear the *dhuku* for public occasions, such as weddings or funerals, and remove them indoors. Turbans identify family lineage, social status and whether one is eligible to be married. The manner in which a *gele* is tied, for example, indicates marital status. An end leaning to the left means 'I am single,' and to the right 'I am wed.' The turbans can be elaborate, large and gravity-defying. They keep hairstyles protected and lend elegance even for everyday wear. The headwraps are often worn for religious occasions. For instance, at funerals the Tonga people of Zambia wear the *dhukus* downwards, whereas at celebrations, such as weddings, they lift upwards. Yoruba women's headwraps often match their garments.

Tilly Willis, *To the Island*, 1998, oil on canvas.

To fashion a *gele* is to make a sculpture. In Nigeria, a robe, shirt, shawl and *gele* constitute a woman's attire for social and formal events. A rectangle of fabric can be used to wrap a *gele*, whether traditional handwoven cloth or a thin, crisp imported cloth amenable to folding, wrapping and layering these intricate, towering styles. The fabric is usually drawn to a heightened pile on top of the head, leaving the forehead visible. It may be all tied, or tied on a base and stitched down. Says a Nigerian woman living in the United States, 'I learned to tie my *gele* from watching my mother, but these days you can hire a professional to do the job. It's a big business, especially for weddings.'[16] Using starched cotton, *geles* are tied in creative ways, such as modelling the designs of Nigeria's first skyscraper or the peaked roof of the National Theatre. The inside is sometimes padded with paper for height.

Wherever they are worn, turbans send a message of difference, independence and allegiance to origins. Women in African diasporas worldwide proclaim their beauty and improvise personal fashion with colourful turban-like headdresses. On their heads, the turban survives in Europe and the Americas.

8

Cultural Tourism and Authenticity since 1900

Vivekananda was an early turbaned religious leader to arrive in the West. In 1912 another turban in-the-round arrived in England and then the United States from the Holy Land. The Bahá'í Faith began in Iran in the 1840s as a messianic religion based on the revelations of Ali Muhammad, known as the Báb (Gate), and Husayn Alí Nuri, known as Bahá'u'lláh. In 1850 Naser al-Din Shah executed the Báb and exiled Bahá'u'lláh and some of his followers to Acca, Palestine, then under Ottoman rule. As holy men, the Báb wore a turban and Bahá'u'lláh a *taj*, or tall cap. Bahá'u'lláh's son Abdul-Bahá Abbas assumed leadership of the Bahá'í community in 1892, when his father died. Abdul-Bahá always wore a turban, an Arab headdress appropriate to his religious status in Palestine, and beard. In 1908 the Young Turks seized power from the Ottoman sultan and freed the Bahá'ís in Acca. By this time the Bahá'í Faith had spread to Europe and America.

In 1911–12 Abdul-Bahá made his first visit to Europe and then to the United States. In his eight months in the States, he gave four hundred talks to seekers in churches (and one synagogue), lecture halls and homes of prominent Bahá'ís from coast to coast. Everywhere he went he dressed in a traditional robe and white turban, complementing his white beard. He stressed the East as the source of his father's revelation, and signalled the West as being receptive to the revelation. Like St Paul two millennia earlier, he planted the seeds of new communities and guided nascent communities to a better understanding of the faith's beliefs and practices. But dressing like Abdul-Bahá or his father never entered the practices of Western Bahá'í communities. After his visits to Europe and America, Abdul-Bahá returned to Acca. Anticipating the First World War, he persuaded farmers in the region to create storage facilities for their grain. In 1917–18, when the port was blockaded, the stored grain prevented widespread starvation. In 1918, when General Sir Edmund Allenby sent a special military force to protect Abdul-Bahá and the Bahá'ís, Abdul-Bahá assured him that he had sufficient food to feed the soldiers as well as the local population. In 1920 King George v knighted him, at the time a rare turbaned recipient of the honour.[1]

Almost all Asian immigrants to Europe and the Americas abandon their distinctive indigenous clothes for Western garb, either as soon as they arrive or when the first generation has passed. In the dense Chinatowns of the nineteenth and early twentieth centuries, wave after wave of new immigrants brought their distinctive satins and silks, hats and slippers. As second and third generations moved out of their parents' Chinatowns, they adopted the commonplace fashions of their new neighbours. For a generation some Indian women wore saris as regular clothing, but the next generations of South Asian women mostly reserved saris, salwar and kameez for special occasions, such as weddings and other ceremonies at Hindu temples and Muslim mosques.

Sikh men were exceptional in their adherence to traditional dress, and in particular to their uncut hair tucked into turbans. The founder of their religion, Guru Nanak, lived in the late fifteenth and early sixteenth centuries in northern India. Nanak taught his followers that the worship of God must come from the heart and transcend rituals and laws. From the outside, his teachings look like a mix of Hindu, Jain and Muslim mystical themes, but in the eyes and ears of his followers he brought a new religion. After his death, leadership of the community came from nine successive gurus. In 1708 the tenth guru died without a successor, and leadership passed to the scripture *Adi Granth* (First Book). In the Punjabi language, *sikh* means disciple, that is, disciple of the ten gurus and the scripture.

In the seventeenth century the new community suffered under the harsh rule of the Mughal emperors. In response, the fifth guru, Arjan, created a cadre (*khalsa*) of warrior Sikhs willing to die for their religion. These warriors marked their loyalty with five Ks, five Punjabi words beginning with that phoneme: 1) wearing a small dagger beneath their shirts; 2) wearing a steel bangle on the right wrist; 3) wearing a short undergarment; 4) leaving their hair uncut; and 5) carrying a small comb worn in the hair to keep it groomed. The uncut hair is tied in a ball traditionally called the rishi knot. In ancient times a *rishi* was someone who had the capacity to control the flow of energy (*prana*) in the body. A *maharishi* was someone who could regulate the flow of energy in the body, meditatively and at will. By adopting the rishi knot and the turban, the Sikh gurus shared an ancient technology for how an ordinary person can develop the capacity of a rishi. Over their uncut hair, these warriors wore distinctive turbans. In battle, they managed to survive the powerful Mughals and even established, briefly, a Sikh kingdom in northern India.

As the British took control of India in the eighteenth century, they recruited these Sikh warriors to form an elite army corps, all bearing the five Ks. As the British Empire spread to Hong Kong in the east, to Egypt in the Middle East, to East Africa in the south, and to Canada and the West Indies in the Americas, Sikhs began to emigrate from the Punjab to other parts of the empire. Whether they were of the warrior class or not, many Sikh men wore beards and kept their hair uncut and rolled up into their turbans. To these men, the beards, uncut hair and turbans were more than cultural markers; they were essential religious features, as essential as chanting the hymns in the *Adi Granth* and saying their prayers. Whether they worked as farmers on the West Coast of the United States, as shopkeepers in Birmingham in the English Midlands or as policemen in Hong Kong, these Sikhs stood out by their headwear. On their heads they wore wraps, not hats.

During adolescence, Sikh males decide whether to wear a turban. It's a personal decision, and often a difficult one. On the one side is pressure from older, traditional Sikhs to wear the turban (*dastar*) as a religious marker. On the other side, teenagers are understandably very sensitive to the mores of their peers. In the diasporas of the United Kingdom and the Americas, young Sikhs are usually small minorities in their schools. Wearing a turban invites attention, sometimes the wrong kind. These Sikhs and their families have options ranging from limiting turban-wearing to special Sikh events, such as attendance at the local temple (*gurdwara*) or weddings and birthday parties, to wearing the turban during all waking hours. For an adolescent, the decision looms large. Instead of a turban, some Sikh adolescents wear a kerchief (*patka*) covering their hair, which is tied in a topknot. Some delay a full commitment to wearing a turban in daily life until they attend college, where diversity of religious dress is more common than at school.

All Sikh males who attend Sikh camps or classes at the *gurdwara* learn how to tie a turban in a style that varies somewhat by region in South Asia and by personal aesthetic in the diaspora. For example, in the Punjab, Nihang Sikhs wear blue or yellow turbans tied around their heads in a conical shape. Another Punjabi group wears white in a flat style. Some Sikh youths in the Punjab and diaspora have adopted from the Maharaja of Patiala a turban style that is wrapped to a high frontal point, a regal touch.

Compared to what we've seen of the grander styles of the Safavids and Ottomans in earlier chapters, the various modern styles of tying a Sikh turban usually adhere to a tight wrap on the sides and a peak at the front. When a Sikh male decides to wear a turban in public, his family or community performs a turban-tying ceremony (*dastar bandi*). The young man ties his turban, committing himself to his religion, marking himself in public as a Sikh, and taking the status of adult. As Sartaj Singh Dhami, a member of the Rockville, Maryland, community put it, 'It is not to tell others who we are. It is a reminder to myself who I am.'[2]

The public status can be problematic because of intolerance of Muslims. Many non-Muslims associate the turban with Muslim males in general and with terrorist Muslim males in particular. This is despite the fact that the only Muslim men living in Europe and the Americas who wear turbans are a few clergy and Sufi leaders. After the attacks on the World Trade Center in New York City and other targets in September 2001, numerous Sikh men were attacked by irate, misinformed citizens.

Sikhs have been remarkably successful in persuading various government departments to allow the turban as an official headdress. In 1969 Sikh busmen in the city of Wolverhampton in the West Midlands won the right to wear their turbans at work as drivers and conductors, instead of the regulation cap. Led by Sohan Singh Jolly, fifteen of them threatened to immolate themselves unless they could remain true to their religious duty to wear turbans while working on the buses. This threat continued a long tradition of sacrificing one's life to the faith. After the Wolverhampton Transport Committee dropped its ban on turbans (and beards), Jolly was gracious in stating, 'I am a moderate and religious man and would never have taken the extreme step of threatening my life if they had not refused to listen to reason.'[3]

In 1982 the House of Lords ruled that Sikhs in Britain were entitled to protection under the Race Relations Act.[4] In the same year, Sikhs protested a British Appeal Court ruling that a private school could require a Sikh student to cut his hair and refrain from wearing his turban because the Sikhs were not a racial group and therefore not protected by the Race Relations Act. In 1983 the case moved to the House of Lords, who ruled that Sikhs were protected as a religious community by the act. Similar to the busmen's right to wear turbans on the job, today Sikh judges in England can wear their turbans instead of wigs. This allowance reached the High Court in 2002, when Sir

Sikh bus driver, 1968.

Rabinder Singh was appointed a deputy High Court judge, turban and full beard accepted. In the United Kingdom, similar allowances grant Sikhs in construction sites to wear turbans instead of safety helmets.

In the 1980s the Canadian Mounties moved to diversify its ranks – having been accused by critics of being 'male, pale and stale' – with members of different ethnic groups. This included Sikhs, who had arrived in large numbers starting in the 1960s, bringing to Canada a history of British military service stretching back to the eighteenth century. A scarlet jacket, jodhpurs and brown ranger hat comprised the Mounties' traditional uniform. The Canadian Sikh community insisted that Mounties of their faith wear the turban instead of the ranger hat. An Alberta Member of Parliament argued that tampering with the Mounties' dress was going too far. 'Canada has so little heritage left to protect,' she told Parliament. 'I believe it must be preserved.' In order to better represent the increasing presence of Asians in Canada, Parliament agreed with the exception, adding a three-hundred-year-old Sikh tradition to a younger Canadian tradition that dated to the creation of the Royal North-West Mounted Police in 1870.[5]

Since the early 2010s, law-enforcement agencies in Washington, DC, Riverside, California, and New York City have relaxed their dress requirements to accommodate Sikh turbans and beards, as long as the beard extends no more than 1.25 centimetres (½ in.) from the face. A few Sikhs had served in these departments when turbans and beards were banned, but the new allowances made police careers much more attractive to young Sikhs. The president of the New York City Sikh Officers Association, which has about 150 members, remarked, 'A lot of their kids wanted to join, but they couldn't. And now they can. This country has given us a lot, and now we want to pay it back.'[6]

Although Sikhs have been successful in the United Kingdom, Canada and the United States in persuading government authorities to respect their right to wear turbans, they stand frustrated in France in trying to get driving licences without doffing their turbans for the photos. France has a strong tradition of secularism (*laicité*), which keeps religious beliefs and practices out of civil laws and is generally held to be embodied in Article 1 of the French Constitution. The French government gives the Sikh turban the same status as the Muslim hijab: no exceptions in civil law, including photos for driving licences. In the official French view, the driving licence including the photo is a matter of national security. It trumps any religious practice.

Although Sikhs wear turbans in all colours and several styles, in 2019 the U.S. Sikh Coalition protested against a blue Gucci turban listed on Nordstrom's website. The Coalition argued that the turban too closely resembled the everyday turbans worn by practising Sikhs. According to Coalition member Sikhjeevan Singh, 'What makes this case different is that this turban is like mimicry. This commercialization of the turban by Gucci is deeply offensive and feels degrading because the turban represents our honour.' Nordstrom removed the turban from sale and apologized, responding to a complaint on Twitter, 'It was never our intent to disrespect this religious and cultural symbol. We sincerely apologize to anyone who may have been offended by this.'[7]

Religious sensitivities notwithstanding, by the early twentieth century the Wise Men of the East had given their name to a vast stock of expertise known as magic. Fixed in the imagination of stage and carnival was the magician with a 'third eye', a jewel at the front of his noble turban. Joshua Jay, a world-famous contemporary magician, associates the turban most with Alexander, 'The Man Who Knows'.

Born Claude Alexander Conlin in South Dakota in 1880, Alexander caught the fever and prospects of communicating with the unseen at a Spiritualist summer camp in upstate New York. Although many in our age look at communication with the dead as an exercise of the imagination, from the 1880s through to the 1910s great numbers of seekers practised it as an art or even a science. Alexander took this germ of a skill to the West Coast, where he failed to find gold but survived the great earthquake of 1906. After a few years of playing small vaudeville theatres with illusionist acts, such as sawing a lady in a box or producing white rabbits from a hat, he discovered that audiences loved a mind-reading act. His went as follows. Members of the audience wrote a question on paper and folded it so that the question was hidden. When his assistant picked up the folded notes, by sleight of hand she delivered to the table in front of Alexander another set of blank folded notes and took the audience's notes backstage. Alexander's turban included a small speaker in a pouch connected to a microphone backstage. As he pondered each folded note, his assistant read one of the actual notes into the microphone. Alexander then read the note aloud and responded. This performance established the flamboyant costume of turban and dark robe as the sign of an Eastern art. It also made Alexander the highest-paid magic act of his time.

Alexander invested considerable funds in producing posters for his act by the relatively new process of chromolithography. Various stones were used for each colour, resulting in the creation of a lithograph that had the detail and brilliance of an oil painting. A poster from 1915 shows Alexander in a colourful plaid turban centred with a large emerald, on a background of green-and-white stripes, deco-inspired, like wallpaper. A poster from 1920 is dramatic: black, white and grey on a red field. The posters were seen across the country, wherever the magician performed. In the 'question-mark poster' (1920), Alexander's turban and end tassel form the shape of a big question mark. Beneath the striking white turban is a striped cap. His eyes look inwards, while his brow is furrowed with concentration. In each design the seer's intense gaze is riveting.[8]

In the 1920s and '30s *Billboard* magazine commonly printed on the Magic/Mentalists page photographs of mind-readers with turbans, and advertisements for turbans and robes. Charles Carter ('Carter the Great') started performing magic as a 'Boy Magician' at a Baltimore Masonic temple at the age of ten. He preferred turbans and robes throughout his career. A poster shows him with a red-and-green turban embellished with a big daisy. Between 1910 and 1920 Jack Gwynne of Pittsburgh worked at a steel company. After hours he performed, and built apparatuses for other magicians, including Harry Houdini. His career lasted more than fifty years. With his wife, Gwynne put on many shows for soldiers during the Second World War. In the 1960s he made television appearances, performed at the Radio City Music Hall and did floor shows, which were not a typical venue for magicians before his time. He often wore a turban and Eastern-themed costumes.[9]

The turbaned swami popular in the 1930s was a successful stereotype on the radio. The mind-reading was convincing enough that

'Alexander, the Man Who Knows', 1920.

some performers became rich. In 1939 the U.S. government cracked down on them for moving to the airwaves, telling fortunes (a practice that was illegal in some states) and selling financial or medical advice with no credentials or accountability. A late example appears in the film *The Wizard of Oz* (1939). In the film's first act, Dorothy has questions for a travelling fortune-teller, Professor Marvel (played by Frank Morgan), after running away from home with her dog, Toto. She knocks at the door of his wagon. 'Can you really help me?' she asks, and he fetches his turban and sets it on his head. He couldn't be an authentic psychic without it.

The golden age of comic books is generally understood as extending from the 1930s to the mid-1950s. For military 'brats' abroad in the post-Second World War period, this glorious recreational reading could be found at the PX (post exchange) shop on the base, and from other kids. A new family moving into military housing might mean new comic books, which would be read until the pages fell apart. The soldiers who came to the Quonset hut library sat and read comic books, too. They responded to the realm of unfettered imagination and escape within the pages, verisimilitude be hanged.

The character Sargon the Sorcerer was introduced in May 1941 in *Sensation Comics* #26. Its publisher was a forebear of DC Comics – which it eventually became after a merger in 1946 and official rebranding in the 1970s – and it was written by John B. Wentworth and illustrated by Howard Purcell. As the popularity for public entertainment of magicians lessened, the inspiration for Sargon waned. However, a review of Sargon's attributes and backstory reveals a comic-book character equal to any popular superpowered hero of comic lore (despite also briefly appearing as a villain during the Silver Age of comics). A clip from Don Marstein's *Toonopedia* has Sargon in tuxedo, cape and jewelled, tightly wound turban, posed with a wand over a muscular, prone man. The caption reads 'The Sorcerer's Ruby of Life gives him complete command over anything he touches!' Sargon is saying, 'Body . . . Give me the bullet inside you – ah.'

In mid-twentieth-century American pop culture, Eastern costumes became a source of play-acting. In the 1960s on *The Tonight Show*, when he played Carnac the Magnificent, Johnny Carson wore a fancy, sequin-trimmed and feathered red silk turban, like a big round pillow. Carnac was a 'mystic from the East' who could 'divine' answers to unseen questions. Carson would bumble on to the set in his black silk cloak lined with red, and have to be caught and settled by his sidekick, Ed McMahon. Carson, himself an amateur magician, derived the persona from the costumed mystics of vaudeville. The spoof was of

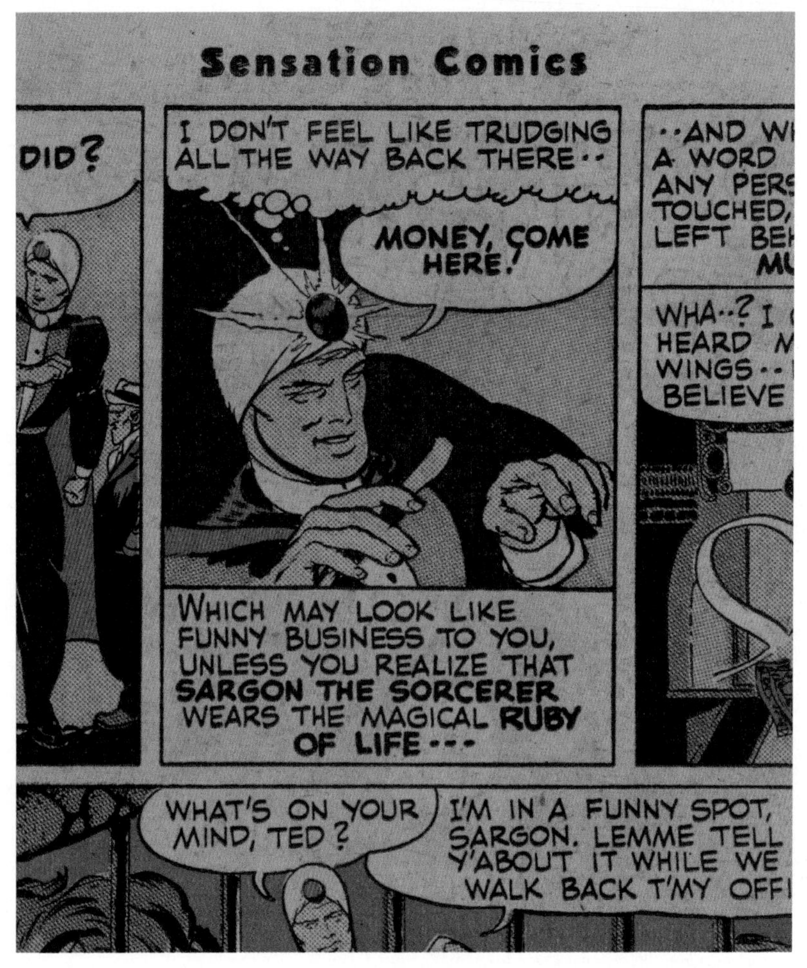

Sargon the Sorceror, *Sensation Comics*, issue 57 (September 1946).

television entertainment supported by an Eastern feel several degrees from reality.

The comedy and magic team of Milo & Roger travelled the world from the mid-1950s until the 1980s, playing their act with Milo in a turban several times the size of Carson's. Milo's turban bounced as he walked. They opened for Mitzi Gaynor and other stars. In context these burlesques were funny, although they would be considered culturally insensitive today. More recently, in the film *Jerry Maguire* (1996; dir. Cameron Crowe), Cuba Gooding Jr as a professional football player dons an enormous, Ottoman-size turban for a TV commercial, but bolts from the set disgusted.

The mystique of the crystal ball and turban, which had begun as a strong pose, became an albatross. Turbans were fading as public taste and credibility changed. Talking pictures took over theatres that would previously have booked magicians. Some magicians gave up, while others adapted to trade shows, nightclubs, television, and private or corporate engagements. A few others could work a rock concert effectively.

High-calibre Indian illusionists P. C. Sorcar and his son P. C. Sorcar Jr enhanced their techniques with glamorous sets and elaborate costumes. The Sorcars evolved shows with the same type of illusions popular in the West but with a Bengali slant, as when they turned a man into a tiger, or made the Victoria Memorial disappear on the three-hundredth anniversary of Kolkata. Still active, P. C. Sorcar Jr wears a purple, pink, green, gold or silver tunic and a colourful sashed and feathered turban. Some of his attendants wear a simple turban of a single colour, such as turquoise, whereas his is vivid with a jewelled brooch identifying him as a maharaja among magicians.[10]

In 1912, eighty years after Delacroix, the painter Henri Matisse travelled to North Africa. Both artists were looking for local colour, and both were disappointed to find women fully veiled. Whereas Delacroix managed to gain access to the homes of Jewish people, Matisse, out of desperation, recruited boys and prostitutes from the street. He painted them in the style of Russian icons, with no evidence of the Mediterranean sun. On a second trip, he found a Riffian male to paint studio-style, to satisfy his Russian clients. He painted him both standing and sitting, wearing a simple beige turban wrapped close to his head and an elaborate robe so intensely green that the colour rises up the right side of his face and turban. The decorative yellow and red buttons down the centre of his robe reflect the many flowers in pots that Matisse painted in lieu of women models. Closer to the streets of Tangier, he painted the extremely abstract *Moroccan I* (1912/13), in which the lounging men have brown faces (with no features) and legs, grey robes and highly visible tightly wrapped turbans.[11]

Back in France, Matisse found his sunshine in Nice and eventually moved his studio there. There his model was Lorette, whom he posed in many guises, including *Woman in a Turban* (1917), in which she sits in a chair wearing a white turban and Turkish robe wholly unassociated with a Turkish harem. The art historian Sherry G. Luttrell speaks of Lorette's turban from a purely visual perspective, as a frontal portrayal with diagonal arabesques of folds reinforcing the whiteness of the model's flowing caftan:

> Whatever colours might have decorated both has been displaced on to the turquoise background and pink chair frame. The insistence on whiteness in such a lover of pattern may be Matisse seeing how much exoticism and sensuality he can wrest from clothing bleached of colour. The turban is exotic yet suggests the intimacy of an at-home, even after-bath moment.[12]

Using North African textiles, Matisse painted fantasies of odalisques in his apartment in Nice, but Lorette is more personal, and possibly more respectful as well.[13]

Like Rembrandt, Matisse filled his studio with props. From a Parisian Lebanese couple, he purchased Turkish clothing, rugs, furniture and knick-knacks. In 1921 he took his daughter, Marguerite, to a fancy- dress party held by the film director Jean Renoir, the father dressed as an Arab potentate and his daughter as a harem beauty. Marguerite described her costume: 'I had loose trousers made from a length of folded stuff, an Algerian muslin top . . . the jacket in turquoise blue silk . . . and the white turban.'[14]

A public revelry captured the attention of Parisians from the turn of the century until the mid-1960s. Starting in 1892, every Bal des Quat'z'Arts (Four Arts Ball) had floats constructed by art students, who paraded on them through the city. This was a headgear free-for-all replete with Egyptian and Greek references but also interpretations of turbans. The outlandish became fashionable. These student balls prompted the stylish people of Paris to hold private parties where women could exhibit the faux harem look in their more subdued fashions.

Couture dabbled with turbans at several junctures during the twentieth century, starting with the intersection of Eastern, Russian and fairy-tale costumes of the Ballets Russes created by Léon Bakst and Paul Poiret. From its first season of 1909 in Paris until the 1920s, the itinerant dance company founded by Sergei Diaghilev engaged prominent artists, composers and fashion designers to create visually striking acts new to ballet theatre. Diaghilev commissioned such artists as Pablo Picasso and Robert Delaunay to design sets, and such couturiers as Jeanne Paquin, Poiret, Gabrielle 'Coco' Chanel and Sonia Delaunay for the costume designs. The company's most innovative designer,

Costume design for a Ballets Russes production of *Scheherazade*, illustration from *Comoedia illustré*, 15 June 1910.

Bakst, came from theatre, not couture. His illustrations, which were used for promoting shows, presented a sensual, erotic atmosphere. He introduced Eastern costumes with vivid, strong, 'clashing' colours. Light, transparent fabrics and the cut of a garment emphasized the wearer's physique. Even if the neckline was low and the costume implied nakedness, the dancer wore a bodysuit underneath. These all-over stockings simulated the natural body but allowed the dancers to keep their modesty intact. Turbans decorated with gems made a dancer look 'more nude'.

In the Ballets Russes's *Scheherazade*, its dreamed-up harem is an ideal platform for the bold colours of an eclectic and fantastical multiculturalism. The sultan of Samarkand wore a turban that swirled and piled up with effects, part Genghis Khan, part Persian, part Balkan and part African, all unpredictably assembled. For *Le Dieu bleu* (The Blue God; 1912), Poiret produced costumes with gorgeous Indian-inspired turbans for a young raja and for the Blue God himself, whose long, thick white beard accentuated the luxurious white turban embellished with large pearls and topped with a secondary asymmetrically tied turban.

Bakst loved to dress his performers with turbans that reinforced the characters' roles. The ribbons or sashes that finished the turbans might have jewels or a web of pearls. A playful interpretation of Eastern culture, the look was big and high but soft, usually with a piece hanging to the side or back of the head. He used feathers, but his signature was Persian-motif fabrics. One turban might be positioned on top of another, metamorphosing a dancer into a sultana or vizier, a genie or a wizard. A single turban might be made up of several different hand-painted fabrics. As Iskender in *La Péri* (The Flower of Immortality; 1912), lead dancer Vaslav Nijinsky wore a turban that built on itself in layers. As if a tall red beret were too simplistic, other lavish pieces topped it, and a paisley scarf descended from a height over the head.

An unexpected amalgam of colours and fabric plus unfamiliar geometry mesmerized audiences and nurtured a tolerance for the

Rudolph Valentino in *The Sheik* (1921; dir. George Melford).

Costume design for the Young Rajah in Mikhail Fokine's ballet *Le Dieu bleu*, premiered by Sergei Diaghilev's Ballets Russes in 1912, pencil, watercolour and gouache on paper.

Advertisement for the brand Fishhats, *c.* 1915.

sight of uncorseted bodies, unisex trousers and peculiar headgear – garments that were taken up by fashionable women, not merely on the stage. In 1912 Poiret brought Bakst's theatrical costumes to haute couture. Women wore cropped tops, harem pants and turbans of metallic and gauzy cloth with the imprimatur of the celebrity designer. Eastern trappings suited Poiret's penchant for draped garments, exotic prints and high-waisted silhouettes. According to his wife and model, Denise, Poiret first conceived the idea of turbans as fashion after seeing seamstresses in the atelier, buried in work, covering their chignons with fabric. Although he claimed that he had been an Eastern prince in a previous lifetime, it is documented that he studied the turbans of Indian rajas at the Victoria and Albert Museum in London. The turbans were a means to vary his designs and complete the look.

Impresario as well as designer, in 1911 Poiret held a party called 'The Thousand and Second Night' for three hundred guests at his home. The Fauvist painter Raoul Dufy designed the invitations, which announced: 'On this night, there will be no clouds in the sky and nothing that exists will exist.' Dressed as a Persian prince and carrying a whip, Poiret welcomed his guests while his wife wore a costume that immortalized the new look. Inspired by Indian miniatures, she wore a fluid tunic over a gold skirt tapered by a hoop (her husband's 'lampshade' style), her bare feet decorated with Eastern jewels, her bodice wrapped with yards of foil. Her golden turban stood a good 45 centimetres (18 in.) above her head and featured a glistening sash around a white cap with a jewelled aigrette that suggested a comet. She welcomed guests into a trellised seraglio, strewn with carpets and pillows. Guests drank two hundred bottles of champagne, and the fireworks that concluded the evening reputedly almost burned the house down. The jewellery and glass designer René Lalique gave a fashionable costume ball the year after Poiret's party. His daughter Suzanne's dress and turban were inspired by harem clothes. The artist Georges Clairin, who was present at the party, later painted a model in the same full-length costume.

Picasso designed the costumes and sets for the one-act ballet *Parade* choreographed by Léonide Massine for the Ballets Russes, with music by Erik Satie, in 1917. The show premiered at the Théâtre du Châtelet in Paris. Picasso worked on his part of the production in Rome, and his designs were influenced by the Italian *commedia dell'arte*. His famous study for the ballet shows circus performers, harlequins, a flamenco guitarist and a winged horse all close together enjoying an evening party. One of the harlequins holds out his glass to a muscular black man, a server whose pronounced white-and-grey turban draws the viewer's attention to his majestic air. He

Fashion model, *c.* 1925.

has a brilliant smile, as if uplifted from the farcical ensemble by the collaborative geniuses of Diaghilev, Satie and Picasso.

Artists influenced by the Art Nouveau style embraced the decorative potential of the turban's curves and twists. Erté used the turban as both a male and female accessory. His first theatrical production, *Le Minaret* (1913), featured Mata Hari, the self-invented dancer of the East. Similarly inspired by Art Nouveau's Eastern elements, Erté's contemporary the American artist Edward Gorey created elegant caricatures of Edwardian high society as reimagined by him. In Gorey's art, a feathered turban identified affluence and pretention or enveloped a beautiful woman in a papery cocoon from which an insect might emerge. Turbans also suited a trim flapper look and led to the cloche hat, which in the 1920s became a symbol of the liberated woman.[15]

European couple in tuxedos, 1920s.

Four men in oriental dress-up, 1930s.

The silver screen became a locus in the twentieth century for turbans. Silent films emphasized sparkle, luxury and the exotic. First there were sequins, then a great use of lamé. Woven from thick ribbons of metallic fibre or latterly plastic-coated fibre, lamé was ideal for black-and-white film. Costume had to carry the story while the audience was reading text projected on the screen, and lamé permitted the most luminous effects before colour movies. Metallic gold or silver lamé was especially effective costuming for femmes fatales, such as the courtesan and spy Mata Hari played by Greta Garbo in the 1931 film by George Fitzmaurice. In a 1923 illustration from the early film magazine *Photoplay*, Gloria Swanson's hard metal turban is paired with her costume of see-through fabric cross-hatched with sequins.

Lamé could push the point that a character was truly a Middle Eastern hero. The plot of *The Young Rajah* (1922; dir. Phil Rosen) took Rudolph Valentino from Connecticut to Calcutta. Raised as a gentleman farmer, as a Harvard student winning the annual boat race with Yale he eventually restores his ancestral regime featuring extraordinary headgear and veils as well as near nudity.

Taking Valentino's place after his death in 1926, Mexico-born Ramon Novarro had a long career in film which peaked under contract with MGM in the mid-1930s. In the musical comedy *The Sheik Steps Out* (1937; dir. Irving Pichel), Novarro makes sport of the Valentino image: a spoiled New York socialite travels to Arabia to buy a horse; she is captured and abducted by her porter, Novarro. He turns out to be a wealthy sheik masquerading so as to get close to her. Seeing him in his silvery turban, she falls in love with him and they marry. Pola Negri was portrayed by the photographer Edward Steichen in a turban that looks like a ball of closely wound silvery ribbon, which makes her eyes hypnotic. 'Her kisses sent thousands of men to their death,' the trailer said for *Mata Hari*, the fictionalized biography starring Novarro and Garbo, she witchy, extreme and dazzling and he in a turban reflecting a shiny metallic polish.

As a young costumer, Herschel McCoy designed costumes for many 'B' movies. In *Charlie Chan in Rio* (1941; dir. Harry Lachman), his floor-show samba dancers wore turbans that rose gracefully from sequined caps and were decorated with artificial fruit and flowers.

Million Dollar Mermaid (1952; dir. Mervyn LeRoy), a biopic of the Australian swimmer Annette Kellerman, starred Esther Williams in the title role. In one scene she makes a swan dive from a platform 15 metres (50 ft) above the water in sequins, turban, crown and

Ramon Novarro, *c.* 1930.

gold bodysuit. Other filmic interpretations of the turban seemed to have gone out of date. For instance, in *Une journée de l'Empereur* (1964), Françoise Seigner as Joséphine wears a girlish granny dress and a jewelled, plumed turban perched over large chandelier earrings.

Costume can upstage plot. *The Wonders of Aladdin* (1961; dir. Mario Bava and Henry Levin) is a European version of the well-known story. It features real camels and donkeys, huge scenes in a castle, bazaar and battlefield, and of course a genie who intervenes on Aladdin's behalf. The film is naive, but the antics of Donald O'Connor as Aladdin as well as the sets and costumes are charming. The vizier and prince wear turbans by the dozen, in red, purple, pink, green and gold. O'Connor's first turban is of terrycloth with a thick black fringe; his next identifies him as a poor widow's boy. Like a barber's pole, stripes shoot around a minor character's turban, outdone only when the

Donald O'Connor as Aladdin in *The Wonders of Aladdin* (1961; dir. Mario Bava and Henry Levin).

heavyset sultan appears on his throne wearing feathered robes and an imposing green turban.

In 1930s France, turbans were seen in daily wear as well as art, theatre and dance. The Parisian milliner Madame Agnès first designed cloches, then came out with draped hats, between a turban and a hood. In 1936 she concocted a beret turban for Marlene Dietrich, whose headgear in that year's *The Garden of Allah* (dir. Richard Boleslavsky) fostered a vogue for pillboxes, tropical hats and turbans.

Pauline Adam de la Bruyère, who took the soubriquet 'Madame Paulette', found her niche as the queen of French millinery during the Nazi occupation of Paris. She had left Paris for Switzerland, but came back in 1940 to reopen her workshop. In 1941 she created for herself a turban to wear out to dinner. It was made from a black jersey scarf, fixed in place with six gold pins. It became known as the *turban bicyclette*, popular at a time when many rode to work and did their errands on two wheels. The turban became the centrepiece of her first collection. It was distinctively daring, with a high drape that pulled the turban off the face and lifted the back section high.

During wartime shortages, turbans were economical, colourful and a little whimsical. Heroically, some milliners, such as Lilly Daché, made them so stunning that they brought the simplest suit alive. Milliners during the Nazi era were required to show their fashions to a review board. Once approved, the designs were reconfigured for sale to consumers. The Paquins operated a successful couture house next door to the celebrated House of Worth. Their turbans were especially notable. They collaborated with the illustrator and designer Georges Barbier and introduced strangeness into their coiffes to the extent that it is hard to take one's eyes off them – as in films of the 1930s in which the well-dressed lady asserts herself by never taking the fantastic bauble off her head. An exhibition of Paquin's work at the Musée Historique des Tissus et des Arts décoratifs in Lyon has a jersey that is

Grace Bradley as Madie Duvalie in *There's Magic in Music* (also released as *The Hard-Boiled Canary*; 1941; dir. Andrew L. Stone).

Gloria Swanson as Joyce Gathway in *The Coast of Folly* (1925; dir. Allan Dwan).

brown, draped with fringe at the top of the head. The tucks and folds look like the carapace of a beetle, or possibly a helmet.

Fabrics and hairstylists were scarce during the Occupation. Moreover, in 1943 the Vichy government forbade extravagant headgear. Cristóbal Balenciaga's fashions for Paris cyclists were an affront to the Nazis, who closed down the fashion house for several seasons for exceeding yardage limits. Parisians experimented with making turban wraps from fabric squares and ribbons, and stuffed the turbans with paper or wood shavings to add volume. Ladies flocked to Paulette's, and small, local milliners paid her the praise of imitation. After liberation, although Madame Paulette designed and made many styles of hat that were not wrapped, every season she presented one new turban, named 'Ali' plus the year. Numerous celebrities, among them Gloria Swanson, came to her shop for turban fittings.

During the celebrations of liberation in Paris in 1944, Moroccan soldiers marched down the Champs-Élysées in elegant turbans. They were heroes who had served in Italy and France during the war. Madame Paulette asked a colonel for a lesson in folding and wrapping the fabric, which she applied to perfecting her own design. Ironically, the turban was sometimes a head-covering for women whose heads were shaved because they had been collaborators during occupation.

Paulette's fame even reached the Middle East. Princess Fawzia (sister of Egypt's King Farouk and first wife of Mohammad Reza Shah Pahlavi), all the three wives of Iran's Mohammad Reza Shah Pahlavi – Egyptian princess Fawzia, Queen Soraya and Empress Farah – and the princesses of Saudi Arabia shopped *chez* Pauline. In countless stores, schools and institutions in Tehran, the familiar official photograph shows Farah wearing a noble-looking turban made especially for her. The look combined European chic with a degree of reserve expected of the wife of the modernizing shah. When Paulette died in 1984, Karl Lagerfeld said: 'She was the last of a line of artists of her time. She had something in her fingers, a magic touch, a knowledge of draping a turban.' Simone de Beauvoir, another resident of Paris who stayed in the city through the war, declared that the turban took the place of both the hat and the hairstyle. She said that she wore a turban practically all the time, 'partly as a hat and partly instead of doing my hair. Washing one's own hair was so difficult you see – there was no hot water.'[16]

Without reference to Paris fashions, in the United States women who worked in factories during the two world wars often wore turbans. An advertisement in the *Las Vegas Review Journal* in 1931 read: 'Turbins! Turbins! Turbins! [*sic*] Lots of them. Metallics and Satins or combination of the two for Dress or Evening Wear.' A drawing pictures one model in a jersey turban and another in metallic cloth.

From the 1940s through to the early 1960s in the United States, Mr John was as celebrated in the world of millinery as Christian Dior was in haute couture. His signature was understated glamour, for which he used not only silks and brocades but Mylar, a stretch polyester developed for spacesuits. Eschewing the flowery and zany, John

Dior turban, 1950s.

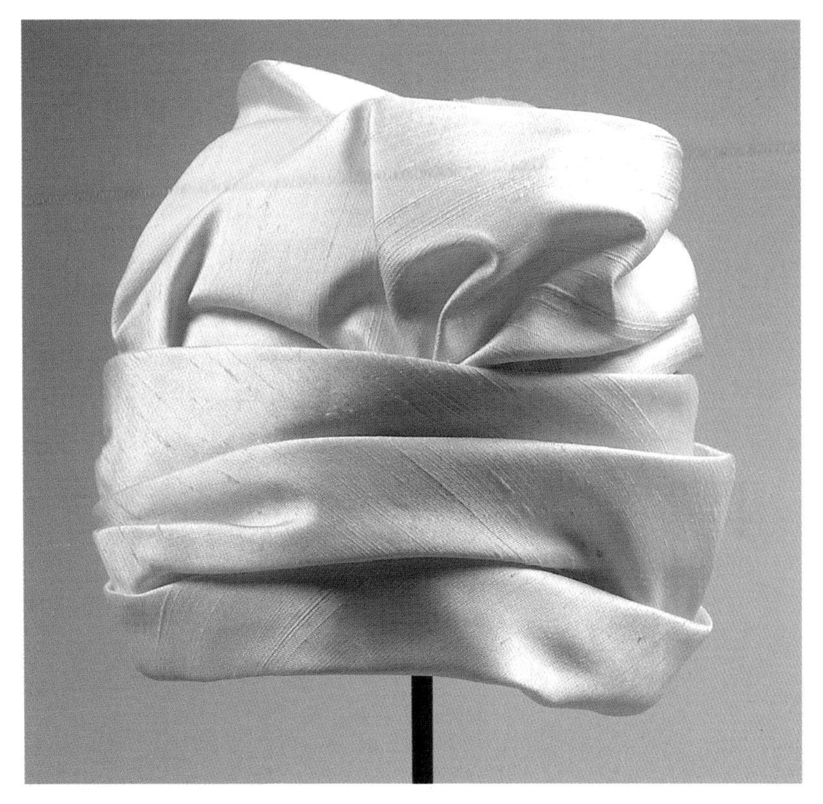

Bergdorf Goodman, woman's turban, 1960s, dupioni silk.

preferred an understated turban shape of undulating folds often set into a ribbon-like base that took advantage of the sheen of velvet.[17]

One of the most intriguing fashions by Balenciaga, a favourite designer of First Lady Jackie Kennedy, was a modern turban-hat. It tended to a bold and abstract design, and is noted in the book *Fifty Hats that Changed the World* (2011) to represent the decade of the 1960s, when abstract art reigned.[18] It turns and turns in stiff spirals of decreasing circumference, mounting the Great Mosque of Samarra. A mouse could climb up it, or it could serve as an illustration in Italo Calvino's *Invisible Cities*. A few years before Balenciaga's creation, the Guggenheim Museum opened in New York; ultimately, the spiralling hybrid turban-hat resembles an upside-down miniature version of the museum.

After the Second World War some high-fashion sewn turbans were worn by Elizabeth Taylor, Sophia Loren and Grace Kelly, the last of whom is sometimes said to have been a princess before she became a princess. She often wore a demure turban. So attired, she didn't have to worry about her hair when photographers followed her on her daily outings, sometimes driving a convertible. However, cloth was also wrapped around the head. In 1949 Eudora Welty wrote an article for the *Junior League Magazine* on how to make and wrap a turban at home. In the 1940s, while a student at Hunter College, Bella Abzug worked in Macy's as a Chanel turban-wrapper. Later, when she was an important politician in New York City, she recalled coming home with arms aching from her day at work.[19]

Queen Elizabeth II often toured Commonwealth and other countries, where she varied her headgear from flowery hats to a variety of turbans that suited her through their delicacy of size, shape and colour. They were of gauze or silk, pastel-coloured (especially yellow), two-toned or dark blue. Some looked as though they had been borrowed from a Muslim friend; others were obviously the cheerful products of designers. Most stunning among her touring outfits was a marigold-yellow polka-dotted dress with matching turban completely covering her hair, worn on a state visit to Mexico in 1975. First Lady Mamie Eisenhower, the fashionable First Lady of the 1950s, often wore a turban in the capital, most notably one of red peony petals that she wore to the nation's Cherry Blossom Festival in 1958. The creation of the milliner Sally Victor, it burst from layers of petals to a pile of blooms on top.

In the last decades of Bourbon rule in France, before the French Revolution, aristocratic women wore towering, self-important hairstyles. A court woman might venture to a ball at Versailles wearing a miniature ship or a scene from a recent military triumph. Such extravagant headgear was reprised later in showgirl extravaganzas at Paris music halls, where it was combined with the exposure of the female body to market 'Gay Paree'. Nudity was an expectation of the shows at the Folies Bergère, but so was dressing fabulously. Every element, including the headgear, had to be perfect in the French tradition of being dressed beautifully in feminine lingerie. Naturally, nudity on stage drew the eyes of the audience, but having the showgirl wear high heels and a feathered turban added excitement to the body. The feathery turbans lent themselves to a choreography of movement and colour.

Mistinguett, a leading music-hall star of the Jazz Era, was so covered in fur and feathers that she appeared to be 'all legs' when she sang – which was the idea, since she was famous for her leggy figure. Tall turbans with an internal structure that kept them on her head made her taller. She encased one of them in a mass of grape leaves and vines. Another featured five 1.2-metre (4 ft) protruding metal rays supporting a superstructure of garlands and wraps that filled a large part of the stage. Moulded to the crest of the eyebrows, these exaggerated headdresses, when combined with false lashes, also made the eyes look bigger.

Backstage at music halls, a turban was also appropriate for a *danseuse* to don before entertaining male admirers in her dressing room. Colette – a performer before becoming a best-selling novelist – favoured the panache a little turban gave her. The North African look was in vogue during the Art Deco era, so that dancers off-stage might change into turbans and zouave trousers.

On the New York stage, meanwhile, the Ziegfeld Follies featured turbans that sparkled with exoticism and provided a zany foundation for the glamour of swaying feathers associated with myths of the East. In the 1950s the choreographer and producer Donn Arden moved two outstanding Parisian music halls, the Lido and the Folies Bergère, to Las Vegas. He had organized entertainment for the U.S. troops, and was engaged to stay on in Paris and Las Vegas as a producer of revues. He continued to have a distinguished career in the second half of the twentieth century. The Lido shows were held at the Stardust Casino and Hotel and the Folies Bergère at the Tropicana

Costume design drawing by Pete Menefee, stylized robe with turban and peacock for the performance of Samson and Delilah in the show *Jubilee!*, MGM Grand Hotel and Casino, Las Vegas, 5 June 1980.

Hotel. The costumes, jewels and feathers travelled with the productions and cast from Paris to Vegas. Cap-type turbans made the performers look taller, and jewelled brassieres and low-slung belts continued to tease the male gaze. Michel Gyarmathy, costume designer and long-time director of the Folies, created turbans as strong as iron to hold up the enormous display of feathers and jewels. The contemporary designer Pete Menefee costumed two dancers as exotic twin birds in feathery turbaned designs (twinness being a vintage showgirl illusion) for a theatrical scene set on the *Titanic* the evening before it sank. When the Folies Bergère and Lido were performing in Las Vegas, the costumes had to be more sensational as the stages grew larger. Turbans continued to serve as a base, for instance, for a giant bouquet of feathers and pompoms surmounted by extra-long bunny ears in the show *Fascination* in 1967. Although supported by a metal structure, the turbans had to appear fluid, lest the dancers look like sentries.

In 2000 the costume designer Jerry Jackson figured out how to make lighter turbans. The fashion historian Karan Feder explains:

> The foundational skullcaps were built from buckram. Buckram was then covered with various layers of textile fabrics like poly-velvet to create a comfortable item to wear on the head. He [Jackson] covered a laser-cut plastic brim with polyester batting and then with knit velvet. The laser-cut plastic discs came in two sizes, a super-large one for prancing, parading showgirls, and a smaller one worn by female dancers on swings, where the designer had less breadth of dimension to work with. The turbans had chinstraps.[20]

The frame story and other tales of the *Arabian Nights* were ready-made theatre, and from those tales costume designers plucked birds in flight, magic lamps and flowing, jewel-studded costumes for theatrical illusions. In the Bing Crosby/Bob Hope 'Road' pictures (1940–62), set mostly in a fantasy East, men dressed as pashas. When the Sands Corporation operated the Dunes casino in Las Vegas in the mid-1950s with Arabian Nights themes, a bevy of flirtatious chorus girls doted on Frank Sinatra who was wearing a turban. A publicity photograph shows the singer dolled up like Prince Rupert in the Jan Lievens painting *Boy in Cape and Turban*, in a white turban with a jewel and a tall feather like the prince's bird of paradise. Sinatra may have been singing one of his hits, 'Sheik of Araby'.

Carmen Miranda, who grew up in Rio de Janeiro, brought the samba and flamboyant costumes to the United States in 1939, when the Brazilian look was popular. Her turbans were *sui generis*: playful concoctions of fabric with artificial fruit and flowers. Exposing her muscular midriff gave her sex appeal, and the heavy headgear made her fantastical. She introduced to Brazilian folk music the songs and costumes of the women of Bahia in the northeast of the country who sold produce and hot dishes. They are known as *baianas*, and their costume *de Acarajé*. During slavery women had sold the delicacy among their wares in the street markets in order to buy their freedom or that of someone else. Their traditional costume was white cotton trousers with a long, flowing, lacy skirt, a lace bodice, a bead necklace and an indispensable high cotton turban. The costume paid tribute to the Afro-Brazilian religious sect called Candomblé, which came from Nigeria, Benin and Bantu Africa with enslaved people. The *baianas* helped to finance their Candomblé houses, and the costume was perfect for dancing.

For some of her Brazilian movies, Miranda – who had been a milliner in her youth – designed and made her own turbans. They were wildly coloured and bore artificial or real tropical fruit decorated with flowers and butterflies. For her first hit film in Brazil, *Banana da Terra* (1939; dir. Ruy Costa), she donned a stylized version of what the market women wore: a lamé skirt covered with sequins, and carrying a basket of fruit. Richard Avedon photographed Miranda wearing a tall turban with artificial butterflies perched on it. At that time she was the highest-paid actress in the United States.

As an accessory, the turban is more pleasing to some fashion-conscious people than others, while all who wear it outside the traditional cultures of its origin are displaying a degree of personal power or overcoming uncertainty about that power as well as their aesthetic taste. Starting as a costume in films with an Eastern setting, turbans have moved beyond the film industry to become an important item of headwear. Female stars such as Lana Turner, Greta Garbo, Angela Bassett, Sophia Loren, Eartha Kitt and Shirley MacLaine drew attention to their beauty by wearing turbans off-screen. Elizabeth Taylor was most faithful to the turban, which gave her a more statuesque look. Taylor wore a marigold-yellow chiffon-and-silk evening gown and a bodice and turban ablaze in blue, pink, yellow, orange and gold, with all-over sequins, paillettes and bugle beads. Her next-to-last wedding was a quiet ceremony on the Virginia farm of John Warner, the groom, soon to be a U.S. senator. Taylor wore a silver fox coat, lavender cashmere dress and turban wound of shades of lavender and purple cashmere to match the dress.

Female singers have also punched up their glamour on stage by wearing this exotic accessory. As the 1960s wore on, the soul and folk singer Nina Simone became more identified with turbans when she performed, and in 2021 Beyoncé dazzled in an extravagant trained gown covered with silver sequins, with a silver sequin-covered turban, at a Grammys after-party.

In James M. Cain's novel, *The Postman Always Rings Twice* (1934), Cora Smith is 'commonplace but sexy, the kind you have ideas about'.[21] In the 1946 film adaptation by Tay Garnett, Lana Turner as Cora first appears when she descends from her bedroom wearing a plain cotton turban to protect her hair. The rest of her yearns not only to break free from her marriage to Nick, but to take ownership of his diner. In the 1990 film adaptation of Carrie Fisher's autofiction *Postcards from the Edge* (1987), Shirley MacLaine has the role of the celebrity

Carmen Miranda in *That Night in Rio* (1941; dir. Irving Cummings).

Lana Turner as Cora Smith in *The Postman Always Rings Twice* (1946; dir. Tay Garnett).

mother, loosely based on Fisher's mother Debbie Reynolds. In the film, directed by Mike Nichols, the mother, Doris, is in an accident and taken to hospital, where reporters gather in the lobby to photograph the ageing star. Her daughter, Suzanne, played by Meryl Streep, finds her in her hospital room without make-up and wearing a wig to cover her sparse hair. Suzanne applies her mother's eyelashes and make-up, and wraps Doris's pink scarf as a turban around her head. Instant glamour. Still in a hospital gown, the mother wraps herself in a fur coat and promenades down the corridor to greet and engage the adoring reporters.

The fluid fashions of the 1930s served as inspiration for many fashion designers later. Typically, the turban adorned a woman of mature and cool affect, such as Marlene Dietrich. Beginning in the 1960s, Yves Saint Laurent paired turbans with fluid, billowing romantic gowns. It's no surprise that elements of the cultures of North Africa and the Middle East appeared in his clothes. He was born and grew up in Oran, Algeria, and later had houses in Morocco. In the 1960s he often matched a turban as an integral part to a dress. For example he created a structured white brocade tunic with an elegant tunic of similar cloth; the effect was elegant and sombre of a Mughal prince.

During the 1970s Biba, Halston and Emanuel Ungaro presented updated versions of the turban on the catwalk. The turban proved to be a significant complement to the inherent theatricality of the discothèque. The Orientalist turban evoked a mystery and remoteness that went with the arty exclusivity of Studio 54 and glam disco. Mick Jagger and his stylish wife, Bianca Jagger, personified a hedonistic late 1970s look. She wore turbans by such designers as Miuccia Prada, which contrasted with assertive micro-minis and décolletage. Karan Feder comments, 'I suspect, due to the sheer number of photos made of her at the nightclub Studio 54, that there is the most intense visual memory of Jagger's turban-clad self of all the celebrities who adopted it.'[22] In 1956 Andy Warhol – ever a predictor of fashion – made a cunning watercolour entitled *Cat with Turban*. The cat looks amused with itself. Its turban is delicately sketched and formed of two lengths of entwined fabric, white and paisley. When Warhol was a habitué of Studio 54, he often appeared with Bianca Jagger.

When twentieth-century designers flirted with turbans, the arbiter of fashion Diana Vreeland was behind them. Bettina Ballard, a *Vogue* editor who preceded Vreeland, described the latter's living

Joan Crawford, *c.* 1940.

room as 'an over-crowded seraglio'. Turquerie captivated Vreeland in the 1960s. That turbans and caftans were originally for men only made them more exciting to her as womenswear. Her first issue as editor-in-chief of *Vogue* (January 1963) featured filmy sports clothes among Tunisian camels, and she devoted twelve pages of fashions inspired by Scheherazade in such colours as hot pink and mint-green. Her haute-couture models walked the runway in silky clothes and turbans. She drew direct influence from the paintings of Jean-Étienne Liotard and the costumes of the Ballets Russes. Redolent of escape and fantasy, the clothes were to be contemporary yet also, as written in the *Vogue* editorial of 15 April 1965, meant to 'charm the sheik at home'. Vreeland was photographed in turbans about town, famously one dotted with stars. In March 1966 she commissioned Richard Avedon to photograph Barbra Streisand in voluminous pale silk-chiffon pyjamas by Dior and a tall, dark turban, looking eerily like a seventeenth-century painting.

The turban functioned as a practical fashion for celebrities who were routinely photographed. They did not have to think how their hair would look in a candid shot, and the style rendered a sense of privacy. When a *New Yorker* reporter arrived at her hotel at 1 p.m. to interview Edith Piaf before her first American concert, he woke her. She thanked him, because she had forgotten to set her alarm clock. While he waited in her living room, the singer changed into interview clothes, including a turban. In the interview, Piaf allayed the reporter's worry that she would make her songs sunny for an American audience.[23] Stars who created a personal ensemble with a turban were rarer. When the pin-up and actor Jane Russell began a line of sportswear pieces called Jane's Way, including skirts, trousers and reversible jackets, each piece of clothing had a matching turban. For the premier of *Cabaret* in 1972, Liza Minnelli appeared in a long white dress, false eyelashes, bright red lips and a turban.

An essentially conservative item of dress, the turban provides an element of elegant balance in glamorous outfits. Although forming

Tracee Ellis Ross wearing a black turban hat at the Golden Globes, 2018.

bright spots on the runway, the turban of silk, cotton or cashmere stops short of grabbing the limelight. It remains a classic and accessorizing style that can be adopted for gender-free fashions, such as the Marc Jacobs pinstriped suits from 2018, matched with turbans tightly wound on the head and surmounted by flowerlike twists created by the British milliner Stephen Jones. Since 2010 turbans have emerged as accessories in the collections of innovative designers, as well as single fashions. Satin turbans can be dramatically paired with trendsetting tailored modes, and royalty – notably the former Queen of the Netherlands – still wear them. A cameo comeback was described by Eric Wilson in the *New York Times* in 2007: 'There are reasons to raise a sceptical brow when a group as disparate as Miuccia Prada, Ralph Lauren, Donna Karan, Marc Jacobs and Madonna attempt to bring turbans of old Hollywood variety back into fashion.'[24]

Jones has created turbans, one more elegant than the next, for decades. He designed the fashion ensemble worn by Kate Moss for the 'Model as Muse' Metropolitan Museum Fashion Institute gala in 2009, a one-shoulder toga whose draped portion echoes the wrap of a turban. The turban itself was of white silk brocade with a pleated surface. Paired with silver high heels, it was an ensemble fit for a goddess. In 2010 Sarah Jessica Parker wore a gold silk turban by Ralph Lauren. Jean Paul Gaultier's turbanesque confections of 2011 twisted high from the cap to form an exclamation point, winding off the head. His silk turbans in 2013 were for men, and total borrowings. They were undeniably chic in their tightly wound primary colours, but they were knock-offs, rather than inspired by Sikh dress. In her Autumn 2016 collection Zandra Rhodes channelled Studio 54 in a swishy Persian- and Indian-inspired long dresses with matching turbans, in butterfly colours. Jacobs had a 25th anniversary show in 2018 for which a beautiful petal-pink turban by Jones, accented by a rhinestone brooch, was coordinated with a dress that, like a turban, had flat bands of textile.

If the comeback turbans have a conventional shape, they are sometimes done in unexpected fabrics, such as Missoni's zigzag knits, Jones's metallics and silks with ribbon-like tails, and Armani's intense spring colours in cashmere. They are often modelled by women of colour. In 2013–14 Angela Bassett portrayed the historic New Orleans 'Voodou Queen' Marie Laveau in the television series *American Horror Story: Coven* in a jewel-red dress and turban.

Is the Eastern origin still there in the curves and folds of the contemporary turban? Kokin, a high-end milliner in New York City, wraps and then sews down his turbans, requiring both machine and handwork. His pieces have been sought out by Oscar de la Renta, Bill Blass, Pauline Trigère, Giorgio di Sant'Angelo, Donna Karan, Ralph Lauren and Zac Posen, among others, and turbans are a speciality. One Kokin turban, for the glamorous wife of a prolific film producer, was made of leopard-printed silk velvet with Swarovski jets embellishing every other leopard spot. The velvet was jewelled first, then draped, each stone handset to create a pavé effect. Another, for an Orthodox Jewish mother of a bride, was conceived as an accessory to the wig she was wearing, and matched her dress. The draped gunmetal headpiece had sprays of smoke-coloured jewels, beads and embroidery in shades of grey with vintage silver-grey pearl brooches embroidered in the mix. States Kokin, 'The effect was an Art Deco/ Mata Hari-looking piece; she could have been naked, and no one would have noticed.'[25]

Besides silk, Kokin uses velvet, jersey, leather, suede (both real and faux), kente cloth and linen: 'You can make a beautiful turban with jersey or velvet that is softly structured, but you can also take the same fabric and pad it or use a constructed base that builds up high on the head.'[26] A soft constructed turban using a single cashmere knit stole 6.7 by 25 metres (22 by 8 ft) was finished with a scarf to fling over one shoulder. His shop was formerly near the Memorial Sloan Kettering Cancer Center in New York City.

> We would get women in who were relieved to find turbans and hats that made them feel and look so much better.

It makes a difference to treatment and recovery if they feel better about themselves physically. It's very rewarding to a milliner. A turban can mean something different to everyone. It can be a religious observance or a glamour device. It can have a medical purpose or be a take-me-to-the-hair-salon remedy. I think the goal of every turban has an element of modesty to it, even when worn with a backless gown. A turban does not flatter everyone. It can be ageing and can also look costumey. That said, many

Barbie in green, 1970s doll.

John Galliano's pink turban.

> women and men wear a headwrap or turban that is in observance of their culture or religion, and they carry it off with such insouciance that it is unarguably correct – you can't picture them any other way.

In an impromptu maharaja costume as a treat for his son, Kokin fashioned for himself a turban with jewels and a plume sticking straight up on top: 'To be honest, I wrapped the turban on my head myself, and despite my best efforts, had to re-drape a few times during the night.'[27]

Certain European desserts are associated by name and shape with Middle Eastern turbans: the popular fried cheese pastry of Crete, called the Sarikopitakia; the coiled Mallorcan festive sweetbread the Ensaimada; and the Alsatian Kugelhopf, which has the alternative names of Turk's Turban and Turk's Head, a yeast cake flavoured with raisins and liqueur. According to legend, an Alsatian potter offered hospitality to the Three Kings returning from Bethlehem and the Magi made the first Kugelhopf in one of his large ceramic pots to thank him.[28]

When George and Amal Clooney (née Amal Alamuddin) were invited to meet Pope Francis at a gathering of the Scholas Occurrentes foundation at the Vatican in May 2016, George was awarded a medal for his work in the field of human rights. He wore a formal black suit and tie, and Amal a modest black lace Versace atelier dress and Jimmy Choo heels. But when greeting the Pope, Amal's ensemble made news in a departure from the centuries-old tradition of a lace mantilla on the head; instead, she wore a turban-hat, suggesting the internationalism of the Clooneys' human-rights work and of her Lebanese Druze ancestors, dating back to the sixteenth century.

Some of the most decorative and clever costumes have been for dolls. Karan Feder offers a celebration in the relationship between the fashion runway and the toy aisle in *Barbie Takes the Catwalk: A Style Icon's History in Fashion* (2023). In her examination of Barbie's sartorial canon, Feder highlights two turbans found in the doll's closet. Both are fashionable expressions of the 1970s revival headwear trend; Barbie's wardrobe is ultra-chic and realistic. The turban-like hats were created on a knit skull cap. To this were attached filaments often used for spaghetti straps on dresses. The styling created a doll-size version that looked like the life-size turban silhouette. Feder curated a touring exhibition in 2022 that highlighted the cultural reasons behind fashions for Barbie: 'Barbie never embraced punk, but she did go clubbing. The turban, a look that started to be glamorous in the 1930s, became disco trend and was adopted by Barbie. The adults knew how Bianca Jagger looked as she came out of Studio 54.'[29]

As clothing, the turban's historical niche is small but adaptable and persistent. Moving out of the Arabian Peninsula into the Caucasus a millennium ago, turbans took on new cultural identities and royal splendour. A trademark of the Ottomans, large and jewelled, they caught the attention first of traders and diplomats and then of artists. In Europe turbans became high fashion, first for men and soon after for women. In high political circles Madame de Staël, Princess Victoria and Dolley Madison wore them. As popular culture embraced turbans, they graced the heads of film stars such as Carmen Miranda, Grace Kelly and Elizabeth Taylor, both on and off camera. Turbans now appear in the West in the daily life of African and Sikh diasporas and other fashion-conscious people familiar with how a turban is wound as well as worn.

REFERENCES

Introduction

1 Reinhart Demozy, *Dictionnaire détaillé des noms des vetements chez les Arabes* (Beirut, 1969), pp. 307, 309–10.
2 Joseph Topek, Director Emeritus, Hillel Foundation for Jewish Life at Stony Brook University, email interview with the author, 5 November 2021.
3 Al-Bukhari, *The Translation of the Meanings of the Sahih al-Bukhari, Arabic-English* (Lahore, 1983), vol. VII, pp. 468–70.
4 *Oxford English Dictionary*, 'turban, n.', accessed online 17 January 2023.
5 John Rodenbeck, 'Dressing Native', in *Unfolding the Orient: Travellers in Egypt and the Near East*, ed. Paul Starkey and Janet Starkey (Reading, 2001), p. 74.

1 A Path into Western Iconography

1 C. Meredith Jones, 'The Conventional Saracen of the Songs of Geste', *Speculum*, XVII/2 (April 1942), pp. 201–25. On Dante, see John Tolan, *Faces of Muhammad: Western Perceptions of the Prophet of Islam from the Middle Ages to Today* (Princeton, NJ, 2019), p. 65.
2 Debra Strickland, *Saracens, Demons, and Jews: Making Monsters in Medieval Art* (Princeton, NJ, 2003), ch. 4.
3 Ruth Mellinkoff, *Outcasts: Signs of Otherness in Northern European Art of the Late Middle Ages* (Berkeley, CA, 1993), vol. II, pl. iii.36, vi.12.
4 See 'Image Assignment: A Journey (303/415)', at the blog Analepsis, https://analepsis.org, accessed 5 April 2024.
5 Ibn Battuta, *Travels in Asia and Africa, 1325–1354*, trans. H.A.R. Gibb (New Delhi, 2005), pp. 67ff.
6 Ibid., p. 274.
7 Kathy Cawsey, 'Disorienting Orientalism: Finding Saracens in Strange Places in Late Medieval Manuscripts', *Exemplaria*, XXI/4 (Winter 2009), pp. 380–97.
8 Joyce Kubiski, 'Orientalizing Costume in Early Fifteenth-Century French Manuscript Painting (Cité des Dames, Limbourg Brothers, Boucicaut Master, and Bedford Master)', *Gesta*, XL/2 (2001), pp. 162–4, 169, 176.

9 John Block Friedman, 'The Art of the Exotic: Robinet Testard's Turbans and Turban-Like Coiffeur', in *Medieval Clothing and Textiles*, ed. Robin Netherton and Gale R. Owen-Crocker (Rochester, NY, 2008), vol. IV, pp. 173–91.
10 Ibid.
11 Robert Suckale, Ingo Walther and Matthias Weniger, *Painting of the Gothic Era* (New York, 1999), p. 91.
12 Ingo Walther and Norbert Wolfe, *Codices Illustres: The World's Most Famous Illuminated Manuscripts* (New York, 2001), pp. 320–21.
13 Ibid., pp. 90–95.
14 Penny Howell Jolly, 'Learned Reading, Vernacular Seeing: Jacques Daret's *Presentation in the Temple*', *Art Bulletin*, LXXXII/5 (September 2009), pp. 428–52.
15 Elizabeth Rodini, 'The Sultan's True Face? Gentile Bellini, Mehmet II, and the Values of Verisimilitude', in *The Turk and Islam in the Western Eye, 1450–1750*, ed. James Harper (Burlington, VT, 2011), p. 30.
16 Samuel C. Chew, *The Crescent and the Rose: Islam and England during the Renaissance* (New York, 1965), p. 454.
17 Robert Withington, *English Pageantry* (Cambridge, MA, 1918), vol. I, p. 40.
18 Albert Feuillerat, *Documents Relating to the Revels at Court in the Time of King Edward VI and Queen Mary* (Vaduz, 1963), pp. 67f, 103f, 456.
19 Chet Van Duzer, *Johann Schöner's Globe of 1515: Transcription and Study* (Philadelphia, PA, 2010), p. 179.

2 Trade, Diplomacy and Depiction

1 José Ramón Marcaida, 'Rubens and the Bird of Paradise', *Renaissance Studies*, XXVIII/1 (2014), pp. 112–27.
2 Richard Rand, *The Raising of Lazarus by Rembrandt* (Los Angeles, CA, 1990), p. 10.
3 Alexander Bevilacqua and Helen Pfeifer, 'Turquerie: Culture in Motion, 1650–1750', *Past and Present*, 221 (November 2013), pp. 75–118.
4 Ibid.
5 Mark Pendergrast, *Uncommon Grounds: The History of Coffee and How It Transformed Our World* (New York, 1999), pp. 3–4.
6 Bryant Lillywhite, *London Coffee Houses: A Reference Book of Coffee Houses of the Seventeenth, Eighteenth, and Nineteenth Centuries* (London, 1963), p. 172.
7 Ibid., p. 603.
8 Quoted in William H. Ukers, *All about Coffee* (New York, 1922), p. 91.
9 Julia Landweber, 'Fashioning Nationality and Identity in the Eighteenth Century: The Comte de Bonneval in the Ottoman Empire', *International Historical Review*, XXX/1 (March 2008), pp. 1–31 (p. 30).
10 Paul Rycaut, *The History of the Present State of the Ottoman Empire . . .*, 6th edn (London, 1686), p. 45.
11 W. H. Lewis, *Levantine Adventurer: The Travels and Missions of the Chevalier d'Arvieux, 1653–1697* (London, 1962), p. 138.
12 Michèle Longino, *Orientalism in French Classical Drama* (Cambridge, 2002), pp. 145–6.

13 Rycaut, *History*, p. 82.
14 Süheyla Artemel, 'Turkish Imagery in Elizabethan Drama', *Review of National Literatures*, IV/1 (Spring 1973), pp. 82–98.
15 Gershom Scholem, *Sabbatai Sevi: The Mystical Messiah* (Princeton, NJ, 1973), p. 872.

3 Nabobs, Adventurers and Travellers

1 Sinem Arcak, 'Gifts in Motion: Ottoman-Safavid Cultural Exchange, 1501–1618', PhD diss., University of Minnesota, 2012, pp. 31–2.
2 Ibid., p. 31.
3 Evelyn Philip Shirley, *The Sherley Brothers: An Historical Memoir of the Lives of Sir Thomas Sherley, Sir Anthony Sherley, and Sir Robert Sherley, Knights* (Chiswick, 1848), p. 65.
4 Samuel C. Chew, *The Crescent and the Rose: Islam and England during the Renaissance* (New York, 1965), p. 89.
5 Thomas Fuller, *The History of the Worthies of England* [1662] (New York, 1965), vol. III, p. 255.
6 Ann Rosalind Jones and Peter Stallybrass, *Renaissance Clothing and the Materials of Memory* (New York, 2000), p. 55.
7 Charlotte Jirousek, *Ottoman Dress and Design in the West* (Bloomington, IN, 2019), pp. 124–5.
8 Nicholas Thomas, 'If the National Portrait Gallery Buys the £50m Portrait of Omai, It Would Be Wonderful to Loan It to Tahiti for a Period', *Art Newspaper*, 1 September 2022, www.theartnewspaper.com.
9 Mildred Archer, 'James Wales', *Journal of the Indian Society of Oriental Art*, n.s. 8 (1977), pp. 66–97.
10 Thomas Moore, *The Works of Lord Byron: With His Letters and Journals, and His Life* (Boston, MA, 1903), p. 346.
11 Letter to Mrs Byron from Prevesa, 12 November 1809, in George Gordon Byron, *Byron's Letters and Journals: The Complete and Unexpurgated Text of all the Letters Available in Manuscript and the Full Printed Version of all Others*, ed. Leslie Marchand (Cambridge, MA, 1973), vol. I, pp. 226–31.
12 Ibid.
13 Zahra Freeth and H.V.F. Winstone, *Explorers of Arabia: From the Renaissance to the End of the Victorian Era* (New York, 1978), p. 45.
14 Peta Ree, 'James Silk Buckingham (1768–1855): An Anecdotal Traveller', in *Unfolding the Orient: Travellers in Egypt and the Near East*, ed. Paul Starkey and Janet Starkey (Reading, 2001), p. 173.
15 Quoted in Neil Cooke, 'James Burton and Slave Girls', in *Unfolding the Orient*, ed. Starkey and Starkey, p. 211.
16 Jason Thompson, 'Edward Lane in Egypt', *Journal of the American Research Center in Egypt*, XXXIV (1997), pp. 245–6.
17 John Keay, *The Tartan Turban: In Search of Alexander Gardner* (London, 2017), p. 126.
18 Ibid., p. 173.
19 Ibid., p. 258.

20 Lesley Blanch, *The Wilder Shores of Love* (New York, 1954), p. 19.
21 Isabel Burton, *The Life of Captain Sir Richard Burton* (New York, 1898), vol. I, p. 153.
22 Blanch, *The Wilder Shores*, p. 71.
23 Burton, *The Life of Captain Sir Richard Burton*, vol. I, p. 304.

4 Masques and Turquerie

1 Nabil Matar, 'John Locke and the "Turbanned Nations"', *Journal of Islamic Studies*, II/1 (1991), pp. 67–77 (pp. 71ff).
2 Julia Landweber, 'Leaving France, "Turning Turk", Becoming Ottoman: The Transformation of Comte Claude-Alexandre de Bonneval into Humbaraci Ahmed Pasha', in *Living in the Ottoman Realm: Empire and Identity 13th to 20th Centuries*, ed. Christine Isom-Verhaaren and Kent F. Schull (Bloomington, IN, 2016), pp. 209–24.
3 Giacomo Casanova, *The Memoirs of Jacques Casanova de Seingalt* (New York, 1932), vol. I, p. 58.
4 Quoted in Julia Landweber, 'Fashioning Nationality and Identity in the Eighteenth Century: The Comte de Bonneval in the Ottoman Empire', *International Historical Review*, XXX/1 (March 2008), pp. 1–31 (p. 30).
5 Ibid., p. 25.
6 Quoted ibid., p. 30.
7 Ivo Andrić, *Bosnian Chronicle*, trans. Joseph Hitrec (New York, 1963), p. 52.
8 Orville T. Murphy, *Charles Gravier, Comte de Vergennes: French Diplomacy in the Age of Revolution* (Albany, NY, 1982), p. 68.
9 Email from Georg Lechner, Curator, Collection of Baroque Art, Belvedere Gallery, Vienna, 15 July 2022.
10 Perrin Stein, 'Madame de Pompadour and the Harem Imagery at Bellevue', *Gazette des Beaux Arts*, XI (January 1994), p. 30.
11 Ibid.
12 Étienne-Léon Lamothe-Langon, *Memoirs of the Comtesse du Barry with Minute Details of Her Entire Career as Favorite of Louis XV, Written by Herself* (New York, 1903), p. 213.
13 Rachel Finnegan, 'The Divan Club, 1744–46', *Electronic Journal of Oriental Studies*, IX/9 (2006), pp. 1–87.
14 Quoted in Cynthia J. Lowenthal, *Lady Mary Wortley Montagu and the Eighteenth-Century Familiar Letter* (Athens, GA, 2010), p. 103.
15 Marcia Pointon, *Hanging the Head: Portraiture and Social Formation in Eighteenth-Century England* (New Haven, CT, 1993), pp. 141–57.
16 Sacheverell Sitwell, *Gallery of Fashion 1790–1822* (London, 1949), p. 10.
17 Elizabeth Salter, *Edith Sitwell* (London, 1979), p. 10.

5 Riding the Magic Carpet

1 Richard Burton, *The Arabian Nights' Entertainment or the Book of a Thousand Nights and a Night* (New York, 1997), pp. 529–37.
2 Ignacz Kunos, *Forty-Four Turkish Fairy Tales* (London, 1913), pp. 87–94.

3 Mulla Nasreddin is a Turkish form of the Arabic Mawlana Nasir al-Din. As the tales travelled through a vast territory stretching from Romania to China, the witty and often wise man's name took many variant forms. So popular were the stories that UNESCO declared 1996–7 to be International Nasreddin Year.
4 *Aarne-Thompson-Uther Index*, type 1558
5 Based on the adapted Ramadan version in Sarah Conover and Freda Crane, *Ayat Jamilah: Beautiful Signs: A Treasury of Islamic Wisdom for Children and Parents* (Boston, MA, 2010), pp. 92–4.
6 Ulrich Marzolph, *101 Middle Eastern Tales and Their Impact on Western Oral Tradition* (Detroit, MI, 2020), p. 474.
7 Everett K. Rowson, 'Two Homoerotic Narratives from Mamluk Literature: al-Safadi's Law'at al-Shaki and Ibn Danyal's al-Mutayyam', in *Homoeroticism in Classical Arabic Literature*, ed. J. W. Wright (New York, 1997), p. 171.
8 Jamāl al-Dīn ʿAbd al-Raḥīm al-Jawbarī, *The Book of Charlatans*, ed. Manuela Dengler, trans. Humphrey Davies (New York, 2020), p. 55.

6 A Neoclassical Accessory

1 John Rodenbeck, 'Dressing Native', in *Unfolding the Orient: Travellers in Egypt and the Near East*, ed. Paul Starkey and Janet Starkey (Reading, 2001), p. 74.
2 John Sanford Saltus, *Mystery of a Royal House* (New York, 1900), p. 143.
3 Pierson Dixon, *Pauline, Napoleon's Favorite Sister* (New York, 1964), p. 153.
4 Leonora Sansay, *Secret History; or, The Horrors of St Domingo* (Philadelphia, PA, 1808), p. 65.
5 Quoted in Hope Greenberg, 'Turbans and Head Wear in Jane Austen's World', www.uvm.edu, p. 4, accessed 1 November 2022.
6 Ibid.
7 Ibid.
8 Conover Hunt, *Dolley and the 'Great Little Madison'* (Washington, DC, 1977), pp. 45–58.
9 Conover Hunt, 'Getting It Right: The Embellished Obligations of Dolley Madison', *White House History*, 35 (Summer 2014), available online at www.whitehousehistory.org.
10 Wendy A. Cooper, *Classical Taste in America, 1800–1840* (New York, 1993), p. 37.
11 Catherine Owens Peare, *Henry Wadsworth Longfellow: His Life* (New York, 1953), pp. 62ff.
12 Delphine de Girardin, *Lettres Parisiennes du Vicomte de Launay* (Paris, 1986), vol. I, pp. 117–18.
13 Adam Geczy, *Fashion and Orientalism: Dress, Textiles and Culture from the 17th to the 21st Century* (London, 2013), p. 75.
14 Ghislain de Diesbach, *Madame de Staël* (Paris, 1984), p. 525.
15 Aileen Ribeiro, *Ingres in Fashion: Representations of Dress and Appearance in Ingres's Images of Women* (New Haven, CT, 1999), ch. 11.
16 Ibid.

17 Timothy Wilson-Smith, *Delacroix: A Life* (London, 1992), p. 103.
18 Ibid., p. 26.
19 Patrick Noon and Christopher Riopelle, *Delacroix and the Rise of Modern Art* (London, 2015), p. 84.
20 Zain Abdullah, 'The Art of Black Muslim Lives', *Muslim World*, CX/3 (Summer 2020), pp. 274–307 (pp. 286, 281).
21 Charlotte Brontë, *Villette* (Oxford, 1984), pp. 317–18.
22 Jeffrey Cass, 'The Turban as Metonymy: Reading Orientalism in Charlotte Brontë's *Villette*', *CEA Critic*, LXXVII/2 (July 2015), pp. 189–95 (p. 199).
23 C. Lawford, 'Turbans, Tea and Talk of Books: The Literary Parties of Elizabeth Spence and Elizabeth Benger', sections 10, 8, 30, www.semanticscholar.org, accessed 25 January 2023.
24 Jon Dunn, *The Glitter in the Green: In Search of Hummingbirds* (New York, 2021), p. 175.
25 Elizabeth Gaskell, *Cranford: The Cage at Cranford; The Moorland Cottage* (London, 1934), p. 122.
26 Shrabani Basu, *Victoria and Abdul* (New York, 2017), p. 46.
27 Ibid., pp. 157–8.

7 Individual Expressions: Africa and the Caribbean

1 Nehemia Levtzion and Jay Spaulding, eds, *Medieval West Africa: Views from Arab Scholars and Merchants* (Princeton, NJ, 2003), pp. 15–16.
2 Thomas F. Earle, *Black Africans in Renaissance Europe* (New York, 2010), pp. 134–5.
3 Simon Gikandi, *Slavery and the Culture of Taste* (Princeton, NJ, 2011), p. 28.
4 Daniel G. LaMont, 'Benjamin Thompson's Farewell (1850)', New Hampshire Historical Society, see www.nhhistory.org, accessed 26 October 2023.
5 Paula Byrne, *Belle: The True Story of Dido Belle* (London, 2014), p. 210.
6 Benjamin Morton, *The Veiled Empress: An Unacademic Biography* (New York, 1923), pp. 35–6.
7 Mary Chesnut, *A Diary from Dixie* (Cambridge, MA, 1980), p. 148.
8 Janet Schaw, *Journal of a Lady of Quality* (New Haven, CT, 1923), p. 108.
9 *Virginia Gazette and General Advertiser*, 4 June 1799.
10 Schaw, *Journal*, p. 108.
11 Louis Hughes, *Thirty Years a Slave: From Bondage to Freedom; the Institution of Slavery as Seen on the Plantation and in the Home of the Planter* (Milwaukee, WI, 1897), p. 42.
12 Email from Linda Baumgarten, 23 August 2021.
13 Carolyn Morrow Long, *A New Orleans Voudou Priestess: The Legend and Reality of Marie Laveau* (Gainesville, FL, 2006), p. 200.
14 Ibid, p. 195.
15 Wole Soyinka, *Aké: The Years of Childhood* (New York, 1981), p. 202.
16 Akua Banful interview, 5 January 2022.

8 Cultural Tourism and Authenticity since 1900

1 H. M. Balyuzi, *'Abdu'l-Bahá: The Centre of the Covenant of Bahá'u'lláh* (London, 1971), pp. 425–30, 443–4.
2 Quoted in the *Washington Post*, 20 June 2010, p. C3.
3 Sohan Singh Jolly quoted an article of 10 April 1969 by *The Guardian*, made available online at www.theguardian.com, 10 April 2010.
4 *The Times*, 31 July 1982, p. 9.
5 *New York Times*, 14 October 1989, section 1, p. 4.
6 *New York Times*, 29 December 2016, p. A21.
7 *The Guardian*, 15 May 2019.
8 Diego Domingo interview, 26 October 2020.
9 Ibid.
10 Krishnendu Dutta interview, 24 December 2022.
11 Jack Cowart et al., *Matisse in Morocco: The Paintings and Drawings, 1912–1913* (New York, 1990), pp. 94–105.
12 Email from Sherry Luttrell, 20 October 2022.
13 Ibid.
14 Hilary Spurling, *Matisse, the Master* (New York, 2006), p. 243.
15 Robert Anderson, *Fifty Hats that Changed the World* (London, 2011), p. 14.
16 Quoted in Annie Schneider, *Hats by Madame Paulette: Paris Milliner Extraordinaire* (London, 2014), pp. 41ff.
17 Anne-Marie Schiro, 'Mr John, 91, Hat Designer for Stars and Society', *New York Times*, 29 June 1993, p. D23.
18 Anderson, *Fifty Hats that Changed the World*, p. 56.
19 Anu Kumar, 'The Hindu Turaban Wrappers of Hollywood, https://the juggernaut.com, accessed 11 June 2024.
20 Karan Feder interview, 28 September 2021. In 2021 Feder created the travelling exhibition *Barbie®: A Cultural Icon: 60 Years of Fashion and Inspiration*.
21 Paul Skenazy, *James M. Cain* (New York, 1989), p. 21.
22 Karan Feder interview, 28 September 2021.
23 *New Yorker*, 29 August 1956, p. 12.
24 *New York Times*, 29 March 2007, p. G4.
25 Kokin interview, 1 September 2022.
26 Ibid.
27 Ibid.
28 Darra Goldstein, *The Oxford Companion to Sugar and Sweets* (New York, 2015), p. 312.
29 Feder interview.

BIBLIOGRAPHY

Abdullah, Zain, 'The Art of Black Muslim Lives', *Muslim World*, CX (Summer 2020), pp. 274–307

Archer, Mildred, *India and British Portraiture, 1770–1825* (Karachi, 1979)

Artemel, Süheyla, 'Turkish Imagery in Elizabethan Drama', *Review of National Literatures*, IV/1 (Spring 1973), pp. 82–98

Basu, Shrabani, *Victoria and Abdul* (New York, 2017)

Buckridge, Steeve O., *The Language of Dress: Resistance and Accommodation in Jamaica, 1760–1890* (Kingston, Jamaica, 2004)

Cass, Jeffrey, 'The Turban as Metonymy: Reading Orientalism in Charlotte Bronte's *Villette*', CEA *Critic*, LXXVII/2 (July 2015), pp. 189–95

Chehabi, Houchang, 'Dress Codes for Men in Turkey and Iran', in *Men of Order: Authoritarian Modernization under Ataturk and Reza Shah*, ed. Touraj Atabaki and Erik J. Zuercher (London, 2004), pp. 209–37

Chew, Samuel C., *The Crescent and the Rose: Islam and England during the Renaissance* (New York, 1965)

DeNegri, Eve, *Nigerian Body Adornment* (Lagos, 1976)

DuPlessis, Robert S., *The Material Atlantic: Clothing, Commerce, and Colonization in the Atlantic World, 1650–1800* (Cambridge, 2015)

Earle, Thomas F., *Black Africans in Renaissance Europe* (New York, 2010)

Ford, Richard Thompson, *Dress Codes: How the Laws of Fashion Made History* (New York, 2021)

Freeth, Zahra, and H.V.F. Winstone, *Explorers of Arabia: From the Renaissance to the End of the Victorian Era* (New York, 1978)

Friedman, John Block, 'The Art of the Exotic: Robinet Testard's Turbans and Turban-Like Coiffeur', in *Medieval Clothing and Textiles*, ed. Robin Netherton and Gale R. Owen-Crocker (Rochester, NY, 2008), vol. IV, pp. 173–91

Geczy, Adam, *Fashion and Orientalism: Dress, Textiles and Culture from the 17th to the 21st Century* (London, 2013)

Harper, James, ed., *The Turk and Islam in the Western Eye, 1450–1750* (Burlington, VT, 2011)

Jirousek, Charlotte, *Ottoman Dress and Design in the West* (Bloomington, IN, 2019)
Kaplan, Paul H. D., *The Rise of the Black Magus in Western Art* (Ann Arbor, MI, 1985)
Keay, John, *The Tartan Turban: In Search of Alexander Gardner* (London, 2017)
Landweber, Julia, 'Fashioning Nationality and Identity in the Eighteenth Century: The Comte de Bonneval in the Ottoman Empire', *International Historical Review*, XXX/1 (March 2008), pp. 1–31
Lawford, C., 'Turbans, Tea and Talk of Books: The Literary Parties of Elizabeth Spence and Elizabeth Benger', www.semanticscholar.org
Lindisfarne-Tapper, Nancy, and Bruce Ingham, *Languages of Dress in the Middle East* (Richmond, 1997)
Longino, Michèle, *Orientalism in French Classical Drama* (Cambridge, 2002)
McClellan, Elizabeth, *History of American Costume* (New York, 1936)
MacKenzie, John M., *Orientalism: History, Theory and the Arts* (Manchester, 1995)
Matar, Nabil, 'John Locke and the "Turbanned Nations"', *Journal of Islamic Studies*, II/1 (1991), pp. 67–77
Mellinkoff, Ruth, *Outcasts: Signs of Otherness in Northern European Art of the Late Middle Ages* (Berkeley, CA, 1993)
Nechtman, Tillman, *Nabobs: Empire and Identity in Eighteenth-Century Britain* (Cambridge, 2010)
Pointon, Marcia, *Hanging the Head: Portraiture and Social Formation in Eighteenth-Century England* (New Haven, CT, 1993)
Ribeiro, Aileen, *Ingres in Fashion: Representations of Dress and Appearance in Ingres's Images of Women* (New Haven, CT, 1999)
Schneider, Annie, *Hats by Madame Paulette: Paris Milliner Extraordinaire* (London, 2014)
Shirley, Evelyn Philip, *The Sherley Brothers: An Historical Memoir of the Lives of Sir Thomas Sherley, Sir Anthony Sherley, and Sir Robert Sherley, Knights* (Chiswick, 1848)
Starkey, Paul, and Janet Starkey, eds, *Unfolding the Orient: Travellers in Egypt and the Near East* (Reading, 2001)
Stein, Perrin, 'Madame de Pompadour and the Harem Imagery at Bellevue', *Gazette des Beaux Arts*, XI (January 1994), pp. 29–44
Sweetman, John, *The Oriental Obsession: Islamic Inspiration in British and American Art and Architecture, 1500–1920* (New York, 1988)
Thompson, Jason, 'Edward Lane in Egypt', *Journal of the American Research Center in Egypt*, XXXIV (1997), pp. 243–61
Trexler, Richard C., *The Journey of the Magi: Meanings in History of a Christian Story* (Princeton, NJ, 1997)

ACKNOWLEDGEMENTS

We thank the following scholars for sharing their knowledge – David Arnheim; Sherry Goodman, University of California, Berkeley Art Museum; Ulrich Marzolph, Professor Emeritus of Islamic Studies, University of Göttingen; and Iranologist Bahram Sohrabi. We also benefitted from the expertise and energy of several university reference librarians – Chris Kretz, Stony Brook University; Cindy Phan, Harvard '24, for guiding Jane through the stacks of the Widener Library; Amanda Hannoosh Steinberg, Librarian for Islamic Art and Architecture, Harvard University; and Cathy Zeljak, George Washington University. To the dozens of interlibrary loan librarians who, usually anonymously, delivered to us arcane books and journal articles, many thanks. This group of librarians has given us and other scholars access to vast book and journal collections outside the institutional walls in which we do our research.

PHOTO ACKNOWLEDGEMENTS

The author and publishers wish to thank the organizations and individuals listed below for authorizing reproduction of their work.

Alamy: pp. 15 (blinkwinkel), 24 (The Picture Art Collection), 25 (The Picture Art Collection), 60 (The National Trust Photolibrary), 188 (Keystone Press), 197 (Chronicle), 199 (Everett Collection); Amsterdam Pipe Museum: p. 107; Art Resource, NY/© The Metropolitan Museum of Art: p. 55 (Gift of Mrs. Charles Wrightsman, 2008); Art Resource, NY/Victoria and Albert Museum, London: p. 200; BDA Photo Archive: p. 94; Bpk-Bildagentur/Gemäldegalerie Staatliche Museen, Berlin, Germany/Art Resource, NY: p. 29; Bridgeman Images: pp. 35, 37 (Photo © Stefano Baldini), 67 (The Stapleton Collection), 84 (Photo © Agnew's, London), 128, 142 (© Virginia Historical Society), 181 (Tilly Willis/All Rights Reserved 2024), 223 (Everett Collection), 225 (Everett Collection); © The Trustees of the British Museum, London: pp. 40 left, 70, 89; Centraal Museum, Utrecht: p. 41; The Cleveland Museum of Art: p. 112 right (Gift of the John Huntington Art and Polytechnic Trust 1915/534); Colonial Williamsburg Foundation: p. 173; Cornell University: p. 135; Everett Collection: p. 225; Courtesy Everett Collection: p. 220 (TM and copyright © 20th Century Fox Film Corp.); Karan Feder Collection: p. 228; Folger Shakespeare Library: p. 46; Henry Ford Museum of America: p. 212; J. Paul Getty Museum, Los Angeles: p. 32 (74.PB.31); Harvard Art Museums: p. 113; Harvard University Fine Arts Library: p. 43; Lagardere Media News: p. 229; The Leiden Collection: p. 40 right; Los Angeles County Museum of Art (LACMA): pp. 6 (Purchased with funds provided by Suzanne A. Saperstein and Michael and Ellen Michelson, with additional funding from the Costume Council, the Edgerton Foundation, Gail and Gerald Oppenheimer, Maureen H. Shapiro, Grace Tsao, and Lenore and Richard Wayne (M.2007.211.979), 10 (Gift of Doris and Ed Wiener/M.75.114.3); Collection Frits Lugt: p. 68; Mattheisen Gallery, London: pp. 98, 159; McCord Stewart Museum, Montreal, Canada: p. 176; Collection of Jane Merrill: pp. 201, 203, 204, 205, 207; The Metropolitan Museum of Art, New York: pp. 42 (Bequest of William K. Vanderbilt, 1920), 112 left (Gift of Thomas J. Watson, 1940); The Jefferson Monticello: p. 116; The Morgan Library and Museum: p. 139; Musée Carnavalet, Paris: p. 101; Digital Image © 2024 Museum

Associates/LACMA. Licensed by Art Resource, NY: p. 213; Museum of London: p. 47 left and right; The National Gallery, London: p. 28; National Portrait Gallery, London: pp. 73, 76, 78, 117; Historic New Orleans Collection: p. 177; Billy Ireland Cartoon Library and Museum, Ohio State University: p. 194; Pera Museum, Istanbul: p. 52; Photofest: pp. 208, 209, 210, 221; Princeton University Library: pp. 51, 168; The Ross Art Group: p. 192; Royal Collection Trust/© His Majesty King Charles III 2024: pp. 120, 160; Scala/Ministero per i Beni e le Attività culturali/Art Resource, NY: p. 33; Staatsbibliotek Berlin: p. 131; State Hermitage Museum, St Petersburg: p. 97; University Libraries, University of Nevada, Las Vegas (UNLV): p. 216; Victoria and Albert Museum, London: pp. 81, 106; Lewis Walpole Library/Yale University: p. 123; Wikimedia Commons: pp. 45 (Public Domain), 54 (Private Collection of S. Whitehead/Public Domain), 110 (under Licence Ouverte 1.0/Open Licence 1.0), 151 (Public Domain), 152 (Public Domain); Yale Center for British Art: pp. 64 (Paul Mellon Collection), 164.

INDEX

Page numbers in *italics* refer to illustrations